THE WAY

Josemaría Escrivá

THE WAY

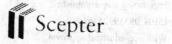
Scepter

To date, 284 editions of *The Way* have appeared, with a total printing of more than four and a half million copies, in 43 different languages; Albanian, Arabic, Armenian, Bahasa (Indonesia), Basque, Bulgarian, Catalan, Chinese, Croatian, Czechoslovakian, Danish, Dutch (Holland and Belgium), English (Australia, England, Ireland, United States, Philippines), Esperanto, Finnish, French (France, Canada, Zaire), Gaelic, Galician, German, Greek, Hebrew, Hungarian, Italian, Japanese, Korean, Lithuanian, Maltese, Polish, Portuguese, (Portugal, Brazil), Quechua (Peru), Rumanian, Russian, Slovenian, Spanish (Spain, Mexico, Argentina, Venezuela, Peru, Colombia, Ecuador), Swahili (East Africa), Swedish, Tagalog (Philippines), Ukranian, Braille (German, Spanish, English and Portuguese editions). Translations are being prepared for editions in the following languages: Amharic (Ethiopia), Cebuano (Philippines), Guarani (Argentina), Norwegian, Tamil (India) and Vietnamese.

THE WAY. © 1954 and 1965 by Josemaría Escrivá

© 1982 by Scriptor, S.A.

Original title in Spanish: *Camino*

This paperback edition in English is published in the United States by Scepter Publishers, PO Box 211, New York, NY 10018.
http://www.scepterpublishers.org.

ISBN 0933932545

With ecclesiastical approval

CONTENTS

INTRODUCTION

These penetrating lines, these concise thoughts are addressed to you, dear reader. Ponder each word and steep yourself in its meaning.

The spirit of God hovers over these pages. Behind each maxim is a saint who sees your intention and waits for your decisions. The sentences are left broken, for you to round them off with your conduct.

Don't recoil: your life is going to be a soothing of suffering. This is why you are a disciple of the Master!

Your worst enemy is yourself, because your flesh is weak and earthly, but you have to be strong and heavenly. The center of gravity of your body is the world; your center of gravity must be heaven. Your heart is all God's and you have to consecrate its affections entirely to him.

Don't rest, dear reader. Always be watchful and alert, because the enemy does not take any sleep. If you turn these maxims into your own life, you will be a perfect imitator of Jesus Christ and a flawless gentleman. And with Christs like you, Spain will return to the old grandeur of her saints, scholars, and heroes.

Vitoria, feast of St Joseph, 1939.

† XAVIER, A.A. OF VITORIA

THE AUTHOR

Saint Josemaría Escrivá was born in
Barbastro, in northern Spain, on January 9,
1902. At the age of 15 or 16, he began to
feel the first intimations that God was
calling him and he decided to become a
priest. He started his ecclesiastical studies
in the Seminary of Logroño in 1918, and
later, in 1920, in that of St Francis de Paula
in Saragossa, where from 1922 he was a
superior or tutor. In 1923 he began to study
Civil Law in the University of Saragossa,
with the permission of his ecclesiastical superiors. These studies did not interfere with
his theological studies. He was ordained
deacon on December 20, 1924 and became
a priest on March 28, 1925.

He began his work as a priest in the
village of Perdiguera, within the diocese of

Saragossa, and afterwards in Saragossa itself. In the spring of 1927, with the permission of the Archbishop of Saragossa, he moved to the Spanish capital Madrid and there carried out abundant priestly work among all kinds of people, devoting attention also to the poor and destitute in the outlying districts of the city, and especially to the incurably sick and the dying in the hospitals. He worked as chaplain to the *Patronato de Enfermos* (Foundation for the Sick), a welfare organization run by the Apostolic Sisters of the Sacred Heart. He also taught at a university academy, and continued his studies for a doctorate in Civil Law, which at that time could only be obtained from the University of Madrid.

On October 2, 1928 God made him see clearly what up to then he had only inklings of; and Saint Josemaría Escrivá founded Opus Dei (in English, the Work of God). Under God's continuing guidance, on February 14, 1930 he understood that he must open up the apostolic work of Opus

Dei to women also. As a result, a new path was opening up in the Church, to promote, among people of all social classes, the search for holiness and the practice of the apostolate, through the sanctification of ordinary work, in the midst of the world and without changing one's state in life.

From October 2, 1928, the Founder of Opus Dei directed his energies to the mission God had entrusted to him, with great apostolic zeal for all souls. In 1934 he was appointed Rector of the *Patronato de Santa Isabel* (St Elizabeth Foundation). During the Spanish Civil War, at times putting his life at risk, he carried out his priestly ministry in Madrid and, subsequently, in the northern city of Burgos. Already in those years Saint Josemaría Escrivá experienced harsh and sustained opposition, which he bore calmly and with a supernatural outlook.

On February 14, 1943 he founded the Priestly Society of the Holy Cross, which is inseparably united to Opus Dei and which, as well as opening up the possibility of ordaining lay members of Opus Dei to the priesthood and incardinating them for the service of the Work, would later on also enable priests who are incardinated in dioceses to share the spirituality and asceticism of Opus Dei, seeking holiness in the exercise of their ministerial duties, while remaining exclusively under their respective Ordinaries.

In 1946 he took up residence in Rome, which was to be his home for the rest of his life. From there, he stimulated and guided the development of Opus Dei throughout the world, using all his energies to give to the men and women of Opus Dei a solid formation in doctrine, ascetical spirit and apostolate. At the time of his death, Opus Dei had more than 60,000 members from 80 different nationalities.

Saint Escrivá was a Consultor to the Pontifical Commission for the authentic interpretation of the Code of Canon Law, and to the Sacred Congregation for Seminaries and Universities. He was a Domestic Prelate and an honorary Academician of the Pontifical Roman Academy of Theology. He was also the Chancellor of the Universities of Navarre (in Spain) and Piura (in Peru).

Saint Josemaría Escrivá died on June 26, 1975. For years, he had been offering his life for the Church and for the Pope. He was buried in the Crypt of the church of Our Lady of Peace, in Rome. Msgr. Alvaro del Portillo (1914-1994), who for many years had been his closest collaborator, was unanimously elected to succeed him. The present Prelate of Opus Dei is Msgr. Javier Echevarria, who also worked for several decades with Saint Josemaría Escrivá and with his first successor, Msgr. del Portillo. Opus Dei, which from its inception had had the approval of the diocesan authorities and from 1943, also the *appositio manuum* and subsequently the approval of the Holy See, was established as a Personal Prelature by his holiness Pope John Paul II on

November 28, 1982: this was the canonical formula foreseen and desired by Saint Josemaría Escrivá.

The reputation for holiness which the Founder of Opus Dei enjoyed in his lifetime has spread after his death to the far corners of the earth, as can be seen from countless spiritual and material favors attributed to his intercession; among them, a number of cures which are medically inexplicable. Many letters from all the continents, and among them those of 69 Cardinals and nearly 1300 Bishops (more than a third of the episcopate worldwide), were written requesting the Pope to open the Cause of Beatification and Canonization of Msgr. Escrivá. The Congregation for the Causes of Saints gave its *nihil obstat* for the opening of the Cause on January 30, 1981 and this was ratified by Pope John Paul II on February 5, 1981.

Between 1981 and 1986 two processes took place, one in Rome and the other in Madrid, to gather information on the life and virtues of Msgr. Escrivá. Following the results of these two processes and accepting the favorable opinions of the congress of theological consultors and the Commission of Cardinals and Bishops, members of the Congregation for the Causes of Saints, the Holy Father, on April 9, 1990, declared the heroicity of the virtues of Msgr. Escrivá, who thus received the title of Venerable. On July 6, 1991, the Pope commanded the publication of a Decree declaring the miraculous nature of a cure attributed to the intercession of the Venerable Josemaría Escrivá. This act completed the juridical stages for the beatification of the Founder of Opus Dei, which was celebrated in Rome on May 17, 1992, in a solemn ceremony presided over by his holiness Pope John Paul II in St Peter's Square. Josemaría Escrivá was canonized on October 6, 2002.

From May 21, 1992, the body of Saint Josemaría rests in the altar of the Prelatic Church of Qur Lady of Peace, in the central offices of the Prelature of Opus Dei. It is accompanied constantly by the prayers and thanksgiving of many people from all over the world who have been brought closer to God, attracted by the example and teachings of the founder of Opus Dei and by the devotion of those who turn to his intercession.

Among his published writings, apart from the theological and legal study *La Abadesa de las Huelgas*, there are books of spirituality which have been translated into numerous languages: *The Way, Holy Rosary, Christ is Passing By, Friends of God, The Way of the Cross, Loving the Church, Furrow, The Forge* (the last five titles have been published posthumously). Another book, which brings together press interviews, has the title *Conversations with Msgr. Escrivá*.

PREFACE

"They are things I whisper in your ear—confiding them—as a friend, as a brother, as a father...so that some thought will arise and strike you; and so you will better your life and set out along ways of prayer and of Love." With these words, which are the keynote of the entire work, the author begins a book whose purpose is to show men and women how to live in contact with God their father day after day.

The Way was first published in 1934 under the title *Consideraciones Espirituales* and in 1939, when the second, longer text appeared, it was given its definitive Spanish title, *Camino*. Since then millions of people, of very varied races, cultures and walks of life, have found in these words of Blessed Escrivá, light and strength to help them recognize God and give meaning to their lives. The growth in the number of editions of the book in many languages—its circulation is now counted in millions of copies—is one of the clearest signs of how it has been received. In a very short time *The Way* has become a classic of spiritual literature, an "a Kempis for modern times," as some have described it.

This preface, then, is designed not so much to present the book as to suggest the reasons for its success.

"*The Way* shows the eternal character of the Church and at the same time its inexhaustible capacity for renewal"—this was how a French journalist summed up the impression the book had made on him (*Le Figaro*, 24 March 1964). This is in fact the main quality of *The Way*: the depth and vitality of its message, announcing as it does that the word of Christ is not something dead but a living reality capable of changing the life of every man who does not close his heart to it. *The Way* encourages the reader to confront himself with the Gospel and so relive Christ's life: "I don't understand how you can call yourself a Christian and lead such an idle, useless life. Have you forgotten Christ's life of toil?" (*The Way*, 356); "May your behavior and your conversation be such that everyone who sees or hears you can say: This man reads the life of Jesus Christ" (2).

The Christian should live "following the steps of the Master" (213), accepting in a responsible way the mission which baptism confers on him: " 'Go, preach the Gospel...I will be with you.' Jesus has said this, and he has said it to you" (904).

The author of *The Way* shows that this invitation or calling does not in itself involve an invitation to leave one's place, to choose another way of life; in fact, for the great majority of Christians it is an invitation to face the ordinary circumstances of one's existence and find there a divine way which must be made holy. That is why Blessed Escrivá rejects the temptation to "get out of place" (832) because this amounts to avoiding the will of God. Each Christian must find a holiness in keeping with his own mission and his own state-in-life; and so the ordinary Christian, who lives in the middle of the world, should sanctify himself and others by means of the world itself, sanctifying his professional work and his whole life.

Human existence is thus set in a framework of faith, hope, and love. The reader grows in awareness of God's presence and learns to listen to his voice which speaks through the people and happenings of daily life. "Too often we live as though our Lord were somewhere far off—where the stars shine. We fail to realize that he is also by our side—always...We have to be completely convinced, realizing it to the full, that our Lord, who is close to us and in heaven, is a Father, and very much *our* Father" (267). "Get to know the Holy Spirit, the Great Unknown, the One who has to sanctify you. Don't forget that you are a temple of God. The Paraclete is in the center of your soul: listen to him and follow his inspirations with docility" (57).

This supernatural message, this telling of God, is not given in *The Way* as a hollow exhortation but as an expression of an intensely vital life: these pages reflect Blessed Escrivá's work as a priest, which began in 1925. The book is in fact made up of passages from Sacred Scripture, snatches of conversation, personal experiences, passages from letters. In May 1933, for example, the author gave a young architectural student a present of a *Life of Christ* on which he wrote a few words as a dedication, and that was the origin of point 382: "When I made you a present of that *Life of Jesus*, I wrote in it this inscription: 'May you seek Christ. May you find Christ. May you love Christ.' These are three very distinct steps. Have you at least tried to live the first one?"

This is one of the main attractions of the book—its direct, conversational style, its personal and deeply human character. As a reviewer in *L'Osservatore Romano* (March 24, 1950) put it: "Msgr. Escrivá has written something more than a masterpiece; he has written straight from the heart, and straight to the heart go the short paragraphs which make up *The Way*."

This deeply felt humanity is not an accidental characteristic of the book: it is in fact part of the very essence of the spirit which pervades it. Blessed Escrivá's main thrust is precisely the statement that the human is not foreign to the divine: not a part of man but the whole man is loved and called by God and therefore the fully Christian spiritual attitude can be described as unity of life.

The above paragraphs have touched on some of the basic characteristics of the book and should help one to understand its lasting value. But these remarks would be incomplete if no mention were made of the historical importance of the book and the mark it has made on the history of the Church.

Since 1928 Blessed Escrivá's pastoral work has found concrete expression in the founding of Opus Dei, that is to say in the task of opening up a way of lay holiness in the middle of the world. Thus, *The Way* is intimately bound up with the history of the founding of Opus Dei although it is not an exposition of the spirit of the Prelature or addressed only to the faithful of that Prelature: it is an invitation to all men of good will to share in the "craziness of following Christ" (916).

During the years when the book was being written, Blessed Escrivá mixed for the most part with workers and with students at Madrid University. It was to these students that he especially dedicated *Consideraciones Espirituales* which, he explained in the Introduction, was written "in response to the spiritual needs of university youth to whom he was giving guidance."

This fact does give us the historical context of quite a few points of *The Way*, but above all it emphasizes one of the basic traits of the book: the fact that it was written facing the world, looking for men and women who want to sanctify themselves in their earthly interests and activities, and proposing a teaching which can be applied to any type of age, circumstance or work: "What amazes you seems quite natural to me: God has sought you out right in the midst of your work. That is how he sought the first, Peter and Andrew, John and James, beside their nets, and Matthew, sitting in the customhouse" (799). "You have the obligation to sanctify yourself. Yes, even you! Who thinks this is the exclusive concern of priests and religious? To everyone, without exception, our Lord said: 'Be ye perfect, as my heavenly Father is perfect' "(291).

At the time when *The Way* first appeared, preaching like this was not merely unexpected—it was revolutionary. Among some people, who seemed to have lost touch with the renewing spirit of the Gospel, it provoked surprise and lack of understanding; for very many more this very surprise was turned into joy: for them the words of *The Way* were a revelation which made them more aware of their dignity as Christians and of the divine mission which, as Christians, they had in the world. *The Way* led many people to live what some years later the Church solemnly proclaimed in Vatican II: "In the Church not everyone marches along the same path, yet all are called to holiness and have obtained an equal privilege of faith through the justice of God (cf. Peter 1:1)...There is a true equality between all with regard to the dignity and to the activity which is common to all the faithful in the building up of the Body of Christ" (Const. *Lumen Gentium*, 32).

Blessed Escrivá's work has left its mark on the features of contemporary Christianity and this book, which embodies crucial moments in his life, is part of that work.

Born out of a deep Christian experience, *The Way* aims at encouraging people to love God and live by God. For this reason it assumes on the reader's part a desire for the divine. Anyone who reads thes pages with any other intention would only distort their meaning by approaching them from a standpoint foreign to the spirit and intention of the author. To benefit from reading *The Way* one must have a minimum faith in the capacity of men to recognize the life of the spirit.

"I am the light of the world; anyone who follows me will not be walking in the dark; he will have the light of life" (Jn

8:12). The 999 points which make up *The Way* were written with yearnings to help us to see this light, so that all the ways of the earth, the ordinary ways of all men, might be ways of holiness open to the hope of the Kingdom which "is not of this world" (Jn 18:36). Anyone who reads it with the same yearnings will not have opened this book in vain.

Note to the Third Spanish Edition

In a few months, the first edition of this book ran out of copies, and the second edition suffered the same fate. The Portuguese edition is now in the printing press, and from Rome they have asked us to make the Italian version soon.

We have refreshing reports—letters from priests, from religious and above all from the youth—about the supernatural fruit that these pages have yielded in many souls. May the constant reading of this book, my friend, help you to straighten out and consolidate your *way*.

This is the request to the Lord for you, from

THE AUTHOR

Segovia, on the Feast of Exaltation of the Holy Cross, September 14, 1945.

Note to the Seventh Spanish Edition

I have been asked to preface some words to the seventh edition of *The Way*.

What occurs to me to tell you, dear reader, is that you place this book in the hands of many, so that our divine madness of dealing with Christ will get hold of many hearts; and that you pray, to our Lord and to his Blessed Mother, for me, so that you and I will meet again, soon in another book of mine—*Furrow*—which I intend to hand over to you in a few months.

THE AUTHOR

Rome, on the Feast of the Immaculate Conception, 8th of December of the Holy Year of 1950.

PROLOGUE OF THE AUTHOR

Read these counsels slowly.
Pause to meditate on these thoughts.
They are things that I whisper in your
ear—confiding them—as a friend, as a
brother, as a father.
And they are being heard by God.
I won't tell you anything new,
I will only stir your memory,
so that some thought will arise
and strike you;
and so you will better your life
and set out along ways of prayer
and of Love.
And in the end you will be
a more worthy soul.

CHARACTER

1   Don't let your life be sterile. Be useful. Blaze a trail. Shine forth with the light of your faith and of your love.

With your apostolic life wipe out the slimy and filthy mark left by the impure sowers of hatred. And light up all the ways of the earth with the fire of Christ that you carry in your heart.

2   May your behavior and your conversation be such that everyone who sees or hears you can say: This man reads the life of Jesus Christ.

3   Maturity. Stop making faces and acting up like a child! Your bearing ought to reflect the peace and order in your soul.

4   Don't say, "That's the way I am—it's my character." It's your *lack* of character. *Esto vir!*—Be a man!

5   Get used to saying No.

6   Turn your back on the deceiver when he whispers in your ear, "Why complicate your life?"

7   Don't have a "small town" outlook. Enlarge your heart until it becomes universal—"catholic."

Don't fly like a barnyard hen when you can soar like an eagle.

8   Serenity. Why lose your temper if by losing it you offend God, you trouble your neighbor, you give yourself a bad time...and in the end you have to set things aright anyway?

9 What you have just said, say it in another tone, without anger, and what you say will have more force...and above all, you won't offend God.

10 Never reprimand anyone while you feel provoked over a fault that has been committed. Wait until the next day, or even longer. Then make your remonstrance calmly and with a purified intention. You'll gain more with an affectionate word than you ever would from three hours of quarreling. Control your temper.

11 Will-power. Energy. Example. What has to be done is done...without wavering...without worrying about what others think...

Otherwise, Cisneros* would not have been Cisneros; nor Teresa of Ahumada, St Teresa; nor Iñigo of Loyola, St Ignatius.

God and daring! *"Regnare Christum volumus!"*—"We want Christ to reign!"

12 Let obstacles only make you bigger. The grace of our Lord will not be lacking: *"inter medium montium pertransibunt aquae!"*—"through the very midst of the mountains the waters shall pass." You will pass through mountains!

What does it matter that you have to curtail your activity for the moment, if later, like a spring which has been compressed, you'll advance much farther than you ever dreamed?

---

*Cisneros (1436-1517): Spanish Cardinal, Regent of the Throne of Spain and Confessor of Queen Isabella the Catholic. Cardinal Cisneros started the reform of the Church in Spain, anticipating what years later the Council of Trent would start for all Christendom. His courage and strength of character were widely known.

13 Get rid of those useless thoughts which are at best a waste of time.

14 Don't waste your energy and your time—which belong to God—throwing stones at the dogs that bark at you on the way. Ignore them.

15 Don't put off your work until tomorrow.

16 Give in? Be just commonplace? You, a sheep-like follower? You were born to be a leader!

Among us there is no place for the lukewarm. Humble yourself and Christ will kindle in you again the fire of love.

17 Don't succumb to that disease of character whose symptoms are a general lack of seriousness, unsteadiness in action and speech, foolishness—in a word, frivolity.

And that frivolity, mind you, which makes your plans so void—"so filled with emptiness"—will make of you a lifeless and useless dummy, unless you react in time—not tomorrow, but now!

18   You go on being worldly, frivolous and giddy because you are a coward. What is it, if not cowardice, to refuse to face yourself?

19   Will-power. A very important quality. Don't disregard the little things, which are really never futile or trivial. For by the constant practice of repeated self-denial in little things, with God's grace you will increase in strength and manliness of character. In that way you'll first become master of yourself, and then a guide and a leader: to compel, to urge, to draw others with your example and with your word and with your knowledge and with your power.

20   You clash with the character of one person or another...It has to be that way—you are not a dollar bill to be liked by everyone.

Besides, without those clashes which arise in dealing with your neighbors, how could you ever lose the sharp corners, the edges—imperfections and defects of your character—and acquire the order, the smoothness and the firm mildness of charity, of perfection?

If your character and that of those around you were soft and sweet like marshmallows, you would never become a saint.

21   Excuses. You'll never lack them if you want to avoid your duties. What a lot of rationalizing!

Don't stop to think about excuses. Get rid of them and do what you should.

22   Be firm! Be strong! Be a man! And then...be an angel!

23　　You say you can't do more? Couldn't it be...that you can't do less?

24　　You are ambitious: for knowledge...for leadership. You want to be daring.

Good. Fine. But let it be for Christ, for Love.

25　　Don't argue. Arguments usually bring no light because the light is smothered by emotion.

26　　Matrimony is a holy sacrament. When the time comes for you to receive it, ask your spiritual director or your confessor to suggest an appropriate book. Then you'll be better prepared to bear worthily the burdens of a home.

27　　Do you laugh because I tell you that you have a "vocation to marriage"? Well, you have just that—a vocation.

Commend yourself to St Raphael that he may keep you pure, as he did Tobias, until the end of the way.

28   Marriage is for the rank and file, not for the officers of Christ's army. For, unlike food, which is necessary for every individual, procreation is necessary only for the species, and individuals can dispense with it.

A desire to have children? Behind us we shall leave children—many children... and a lasting trail of light, if we sacrifice the selfishness of the flesh.

29   The limited and pitiful happiness of the selfish man, who withdraws into his shell, his ivory tower...is not difficult to attain in this world. But that happiness of the selfish is not lasting.

For this false semblance of heaven are you going to forsake the Joy of Glory without end?

30   You're shrewd. But don't tell me you are young. Youth gives all it can—it gives itself without reserve.

31   Selfish! You...always looking out for yourself.

You seem unable to feel the brotherhood of Christ. In others you don't see brothers; you see stepping-stones.

I can foresee your complete failure. And when you are down, you'll expect others to treat you with the charity you're unwilling to show them.

32   You'll never be a leader if you see others only as stepping-stones to get ahead. You'll be a leader if you are ambitious for the salvation of all souls.

You can't live with your back turned on everyone; you have to be eager to make others happy.

33   You never want "to get to the bottom of things." At times, because of politeness. Other times—most times—because you fear hurting yourself. Sometimes again, because you fear hurting others. But always because of fear!

With that fear of digging for the truth you'll never be a man of good judgment.

34   Don't be afraid of the truth, even though the truth may mean your death.

35   There are many pretty terms I don't like: you call cowardice "prudence". Your "prudence" gives an opportunity to those enemies of God, without any ideas in their heads, to pass themselves off as scholars, and so reach positions that they never should attain.

36   Yes, that abuse *can* be eradicated. It's a lack of character to let it continue as something hopeless—without any possible remedy.

Don't evade your duty. Do it in a forthright way, even though others may not.

37   You have, as they say, "the gift of gab". But in spite of all your talk, you can't get me to justify—by calling it "providential"—what has no justification.

38   Can it be true (I just can't believe it!) that on earth there are no men—only bellies?

39   "Pray that I may never be satisfied with what is easy," you say. I've already prayed. Now it is up to you to carry out that fine resolution.

40   Faith, joy, optimism. But not the folly of closing your eyes to reality.

41   What a sublime way of carrying on with your empty follies, and what a way of getting somewhere in the world: rising, always rising simply by "weighing little," by having nothing inside—neither in your head nor in your heart!

42 Why those variations in your character? When are you going to apply your will to something? Drop that craze for laying cornerstones, and finish at least one of your projects.

43 Don't be so touchy. The least thing offends you. People have to weigh their words to talk to you even about the most trivial matter.

Don't feel hurt if I tell you that you are...unbearable. Unless you change, you'll never be of any use.

44 Use the polite excuse that christian charity and good manners require. But then...keep on going with holy shamelessness, without stopping until you have reached the summit in the fulfillment of your duty.

45 Why feel hurt by the unjust things people say of you? You would be even worse, if God ever left you.

Keep on doing good, and shrug your shoulders.

46   Don't you think that equality, as many people understand it, is synonymous with injustice?

47   That pose and those important airs don't fit you well. It's obvious that they're false. At least, try not to use them either with God, or with your director, or with your brothers; and then there will be between them and you one barrier less.

48   You lack character. What a mania for interfering in everything! You are bent on being the salt of every dish. And— you won't mind if I speak clearly—you haven't the qualities of salt: you can't be dissolved and pass unnoticed, as salt does.

You lack a spirit of sacrifice. And you abound in a spirit of curiosity and ostentation.

49   Keep quiet. Don't be "babyish," a caricature of a child, a tattle-tale, a trouble-maker, a squealer. With your stories and tales you have chilled the warm glow of charity; you couldn't have done more harm. And if by any chance you—your wagging tongue—have shaken down the strong walls of other people's perseverance, your own perseverance ceases to be a grace of God. It has become a treacherous instrument of the enemy.

50   You're curious and inquisitive, prying and nosey. Aren't you ashamed that even in your defects you are not much of a man? Be a man, and instead of poking into other people's lives, get to know what you really are yourself.

51   Your manly spirit—simple and straightforward—is crushed when you find yourself entangled in gossip and scandalous talk. You don't understand how it could happen and you never wished to be involved in it anyway. Suffer the humiliation that such talk causes you and let the experience urge you to greater discretion.

52   When you must judge others, why put in your criticism the bitterness of your own failures?

53   That critical spirit—granted you mean well—should never be directed toward the apostolate in which you work nor toward your brothers. In your supernatural undertakings that critical spirit—forgive me for saying it—can do a lot of harm. For when you get involved in judging the work of others, you are not doing anything constructive. Really you have no right to judge, even if you have the highest possible motives, as I admit. And with your negative attitude you hold up the progress of others.

"Then," you ask worriedly, "my critical spirit, which is the keynote of my character...?"

Listen. I'll set your mind at ease. Take pen and paper. Write down simply and confidently—yes, and briefly—what is worrying you. Give the note to your superior, and don't think any more about it. He is in charge and has the grace of state. He will file the note...or will throw it in the wastebasket. And since your criticism is not gossip and you do it for the highest motives, it's all the same to you.

54 Conform? It is a word found only in the vocabulary of those ("You might as well conform," they say) who have no will to fight—the lazy, the cunning, the cowardly—because they know they are defeated before they start.

55 Man, listen! Even though you may be like a child—and you really are one in the eyes of God—be a little less naive: don't put your brothers "on the spot" before strangers.

DIRECTION

56   The "stuff" of saints. That's what is said about some people—that they have the stuff of saints. But apart from the fact that saints are not made of "stuff," having "stuff" is not sufficient.

A great spirit of obedience to a director and a great readiness to correspond to grace are required. For if you don't allow God's grace and your director to do their work, the sculptured image of Christ, into which the saintly man is shaped, will never appear.

And that "stuff" of which we have been speaking will be only a rough, unshaped log fit for the fire—for a good fire if it is good "stuff".

57   Get to know the Holy Spirit, the Great Unknown, the one who has to sanctify you.

Don't forget that you are a temple of God. The Paraclete is in the center of your soul: listen to him and follow his inspirations with docility.

58   Don't hinder the work of the Paraclete. Be united to Christ in order to purify yourself, and together with him experience the insults, the spit, the blows and the thorns...Experience with him the weight of the cross, the nails tearing your flesh, and the agony of a forsaken death...And enter into the pierced side of our Lord Jesus until you find secure shelter in his wounded heart.

59   It's good for you to know this doctrine, which is always sound: your own spirit is a bad advisor, a poor pilot to steer your soul through the squalls and

storms and across the reefs of the interior
life.

That's why it is the will of God that the
command of the ship be entrusted to a
master who, with his light and knowledge,
can guide us to a safe port.

60   You wouldn't think of building a
good house to live in here on earth without
an architect. How can you ever hope,
without a director, to build the castle of
your sanctification in order to live forever
in heaven?

61   When a layman sets himself up as
an arbiter of morals, he frequently errs;
laymen can only be disciples.

62   A director—you need one, in
order to offer yourself, to surrender
yourself...by obedience. You need a director who understands your apostolate, who
knows what God wants. Such a one will

effectively help to forward the work of the Holy Spirit in your soul without taking you from your place, filling you with peace and teaching you how your work can be fruitful.

63   You think you are really somebody: your studies—your research, your publications; your social position—your name; your political accomplishments—the offices you hold; your wealth; your age...no longer a child!

Precisely because of all this, you—more than others—need a director for your soul.

64   Don't hide those suggestions of the devil from your director. When you confide them to him, your victory brings you more grace from God. Moreover, you now have the gift of counsel and the prayers of your spiritual father to help you keep right on conquering.

65   Why do you hesitate to know yourself and to let your director know you as you really are?

You'll have won a great battle if you lose the fear of letting yourself be known.

66   A priest—whoever he may be— is always another Christ.

67   Though you know it well, I want to remind you again that a Priest is "another Christ", and that the Holy Spirit has said, *"Nolite tangere Christos meos"*—"Do not touch my Christs."

68   *Presbyter*—priest—etymologically means an elderly man. If old age deserves reverence think how much more you ought to revere a priest.

69   What a lack of refinement—and what a lack of respect—to play a trick on a priest, whoever he may be, under any circumstances!

70   I insist: those tricks or jokes about a priest, in spite of what may seem to you to be attenuating circumstances, always are at least vulgar, a lack of good manners.

71   How we should admire purity in the priesthood! It is its treasure. No tyrant will ever be able to wrest this crown from the Church.

72   Don't ever make a priest run the risk of losing his dignity. It is a virtue which, without pompousness, he simply must have.

How hard that young priest—a friend of ours—prayed for it: "Lord, grant me... eighty years of dignity!"

You too should pray for it for all priests, and you'll have done something good.

73 It hurt you—like a dagger in your heart—to hear people say you had spoken badly of those priests. And I'm glad it hurt, for now I'm quite sure you have the right spirit!

74 To love God and not to revere the priest...This is not possible.

75 Like the good sons of Noah, cover the weaknesses you may see in your father, the priest, with a cloak of charity.

76 If you don't have a plan of life, you'll never have order.

77 You told me that to tie yourself to a plan of life, to a schedule, would be so monotonous!

And I answered, "It is monotonous because you lack Love."

78   If you don't get up at a set hour, you'll never fulfill your plan of life.

79   Virtue without order? Strange virtue!

80   With order, your time will be multiplied, and you will be able to give more glory to God by doing more work in his service.

PRAYER

81   Action is worthless without prayer; prayer is worth more with sacrifice.

82   First, prayer; then, atonement; in the third place—very much "in the third place"—action.

83   Prayer is the foundation of the spiritual edifice. Prayer is all-powerful.

84   *"Domine, doce nos orare."*— "Lord, teach us to pray!"

And our Lord answered, "When you pray, say: *Pater noster, qui es in coelis...*"—"Our Father, who art in heaven..."

How can we fail to appreciate the value of vocal prayer!

85   Slowly. Think about what you're saying, who is saying it and to whom. Because talking fast, without pausing for reflection, is only noise—the clatter of tin cans.

Along with St Teresa I'll tell you that, however much you move your lips, I do not call it prayer.

86   Your prayer ought to be liturgical. Would that you were given to reciting the psalms and prayers of the missal instead of private or special prayers!

87   "Not by bread alone does man live, but by every word that comes forth from the mouth of God," said our Lord. Bread and the word! The host and prayer.

Without these you won't live a supernatural life.

88 You seek the friendship of those who, with their conversation and affection, with their company, help you to bear more easily the exile of this world—although sometimes those friends fail you. I don't see anything wrong with that.

But how is it that you do not seek everyday, more eagerly, the company, the conversation of that great friend who will never fail you?

89 "Mary has chosen the better part," we read in the holy Gospel. There she is, drinking in the words of the Master. Apparently idle, she is praying and loving. Afterwards she accompanies Jesus in his preaching through towns and villages.

Without prayer, how difficult it is to accompany him!

90   You don't know how to pray? Put yourself in the presence of God, and as soon as you have said, "Lord, I don't know how to pray!" you can be sure you've already begun.

91   You wrote to me: "To pray is to talk with God. But about what?" About what? About him, and yourself: joys, sorrows, successes and failures, great ambitions, daily worries—even your weaknesses! And acts of thanksgiving and petitions—and love and reparation.

In short, to get to know him and to get to know yourself—"to get acquainted!"

92   *"Et in meditatione mea exardescit ignis."*—"And in my meditation a fire shall flame out." That is why you go to pray: to become a bonfire, a living flame giving heat and light.

So, when you are not able to go on, when you feel that your fire is dying out, if you cannot throw on it sweet-smelling logs, throw on the branches and twigs of short vocal prayers and ejaculations, to keep the bonfire burning. And you will not have wasted your time.

93 You see yourself so poor and weak that you recognize you are unworthy of having God listen to you. But, what about the merits of Mary? And the wounds of your Lord? And...aren't you a child of God?

Besides, he listens to you, *"quoniam bonus..., quoniam in saeculum misericordia eius,"*—"for he is good, and his mercy endures forever."

94 He has become so small—you see: an infant!—so that you can come close to him with confidence.

95 *"In te, Domine, speravi"*—"In Thee, O Lord, have I hoped." And together with human means I prayed and took my cross. And my hope was not in vain, nor will it ever be. *"Non confundar in aeternum"*—"Let me never be confounded."

96   It is Jesus who speaks: "Amen I say to you, ask and it shall be given to you, seek and you shall find, knock and it shall be opened to you."

Pray! In what human venture can you have greater guarantee of success?

97   You don't know what to say to our Lord in prayer. Nothing comes to you and yet you would like to ask his advice about many things.

Look: take some notes during the day of the things you want to think about in the presence of God. And then go with those notes to pray.

98   After the prayer of priests and of consecrated virgins, the prayer most pleasing to God is that of children and of the sick.

99   When you go to pray, let this be a firm resolution: Don't prolong your prayer just because you find consolation in it, nor curtail it just because you find it dry.

100   Don't tell Jesus you want consolation in prayer. But if he gives it to you, thank him.

Tell him always that what you want is perseverance.

101   Persevere in prayer. Persevere, even when your efforts seem sterile. Prayer is always fruitful.

102   Your mind is sluggish and won't work. You struggle to coordinate your ideas in the presence of our Lord, but it's useless: a complete fog!

Don't force yourself, and don't worry either. Listen closely: it is the hour for your heart.

103 Those words that struck you when you were praying: engrave them in your memory and recite them slowly many times during the day.

104 *"Pernoctans in oratione Dei"* —"He spent the whole night in prayer to God," says St Luke of our Lord.

And you? How many times have you persevered like that?

Well, then...

105 If you don't keep in touch with Christ in prayer and in the bread, how can you make him known to others?

106 You wrote, and I well understand: "Every day I spend my 'little time' in prayer. If it weren't for that...!"

107   Sanctity without prayer? I don't believe in such sanctity.

108   Following the words of another writer, I'll tell you that your apostolic life is worth only as much as your prayer.

109   If you're not a man of prayer, I don't believe in the sincerity of your intentions when you say that you work for Christ.

110   You told me once that you feel like a broken clock that strikes at the wrong time; you're cold, dry and arid at the time of your prayer. And, on the other hand, when you least expect it, on the street, in your everyday tasks, in the midst of the noise and hustle of the city or in the concentrated calm of your professional work, you find yourself praying...At the wrong time? Possibly; but don't let those

chimes of your clock go to waste. The
Spirit breathes where he pleases.

111   I had to laugh at the impatience
of your prayer. You were telling him, "I
don't want to grow old, Jesus...To have to
wait so long to see you! By then, perhaps,
I won't have my heart so inflamed as it is
now. 'Then' seems too late. Now, my
union would be more gallant, because I
love you with a youthful love."

112   I like to see you live that
"ambitious reparation"—"for the world!"
you said.

Good. But first of all reparation for the
members of your spiritual family, for your
relatives, for the people of your own
country.

113   You were telling him: "Don't
trust me, Jesus. But I, ...I do trust you. I
abandon myself in your arms; there I leave

all I have—my weaknesses!" And I think it's a very good prayer.

114 The prayer of a Christian is never a monologue.

115 "Minutes of silence." Leave silence for those whose hearts are dry.

We Catholics, children of God, speak with our Father who is in heaven.

116 Don't neglect your spiritual reading. Reading has made many saints.

117 "By reading," you wrote me, "I build up a store of fuel. It seems a lifeless pile, but I often find that my mind spontaneously draws from it material which fills my prayer with life and inflames my thanksgiving after communion."

... how ... a weakness or short thick
... away and prayer.

114 ... never of Jesus Christian ...
... never a good and ...

115 ... Figure of ... Jesus ...
... for those who make them are the ...
... We Christian children of the ... grace ...
... and that one is the very ...

116 Don't depend ... with ... solving ...
... a Religion is much more, many times ...

117 ... Revealing ... you who when the ...
... could predict ... but that it always helps ...
... pictured ... that had not and ... and appro...
... surrounds the way ... aright ... which ...
... all my job as well the ... of children ...
... that Elysian ... Communion.

HOLY PURITY

118   Holy purity is granted by God when it is asked for with humility.

119   How beautiful is holy purity! But it is not holy, not pleasing to God, if we separate it from charity. Charity is the seed that will grow and yield savory fruit when it is moistened with the waters of purity. Without charity, purity is fruitless and its sterile waters turn the soul into a swamp, a stagnant marsh, from which rises the stench of pride.

120   "Purity?" they ask. And they smile. They are the ones who go on to marriage with worn-out bodies and disillusioned souls.

I promise you a book—God willing—that could be entitled: *Celibacy, Matrimony and Purity.*

121 There is need for a crusade of manliness and purity to counteract and nullify the savage work of those who think man is a beast.

And that crusade is *your* work.

122 Many live like angels in the middle of the world. You,...why not you?

123 When you decide firmly to lead a clean life, chastity will not be a burden on you: it will be a crown of triumph.

124 You, a doctor-apostle, wrote to me: "We all know from experience that we can be chaste, living vigilantly, frequenting the sacraments and stamping out the first sparks of passion before the fire gets started."

"And it is precisely among the chaste where the most clean-cut men from every point of view are found. And among the impure abound the timid, the selfish, the hypocritical and the cruel—all characters of little manliness."

125   I wish—you told me—that John, the young apostle, would take me into his confidence and give me advice, and would encourage me to acquire purity of heart.

If you really want it, tell him so: you'll feel encouraged, and you'll receive advice.

126   Gluttony is the forerunner of impurity.

127   Don't try to reason with concupiscence. Scorn it.

128 Decency and modesty are "little brothers" of purity.

129 Without holy purity you can't persevere in the apostolate.

130 O Jesus, remove that unclean scab of sensual corruption that covers my heart, so that I can feel and readily follow the breath of the Paraclete in my soul.

131 Never talk of impure things or events, not even to deplore them. Look, it's a subject that sticks more than tar. Change the conversation, or if that's not possible, continue, but speaking of the need and beauty of holy purity—a virtue of the men who know what their souls are worth.

132 Don't be such a coward as to be "brave." Flee!

133   Saints are not abnormal cases to be studied by a modernistic doctor.

They were—they are—normal, with flesh like yours. And they conquered.

134   "Even if flesh is dressed in silk..." That's what I'll tell you when I see you waver in a temptation that hides its impurity under the name of art, science... or charity!

With the words of an old proverb I'll tell you, "Even if flesh is dressed in silk, it's still flesh."

135   If you only knew what you are worth!...It is St Paul who tells you: You have been bought *"pretio magno"*—"at a great price."

And he adds: *"glorificate et portate Deum in corpore vestro"*—"glorify God and bear him in your body."

136 When you have sought the company of a sensual satisfaction, what loneliness afterwards!

137 And to think that for the satisfaction of a moment, which left bitter dregs within you, you've lost "the way"!

138 *"Infelix ego homo!, quis me liberabit de corpore mortis huius?"*— "Unhappy man that I am, who will deliver me from this body of death?" Thus cried St Paul. Courage! He too had to fight.

139 At the time of temptation think of the love that awaits you in heaven: foster the virtue of hope—it's not a lack of generosity.

140 No matter what happens, don't worry as long as you don't consent. For only the will can open the door of the heart and let that corruption in.

141   You seem to hear a voice within
you saying, "That religious prejudice...!"
And then the eloquent defense of all the
weaknesses of our poor fallen flesh: "Its
rights!"

When this happens to you, tell the
enemy that there is a natural law, and a law
of God, and God!...and also hell.

142   "*Domine!*"—"Lord!" "*si vis,
potes me mundare.*"—"If you will, you
can make me clean."

What a beautiful prayer for you to say
often, with the faith of the poor leper,
when there happens to you what God and
you and I know may happen. You won't
have to wait long to hear the Master's
reply: "*Volo, mundare!*"—"I will! Be
made clean!"

143   To defend his purity, St Francis
of Assisi rolled in the snow, St Benedict

threw himself into a thornbush, St Bernard plunged into an icy pond...

You...what have *you* done?

144 The spotless purity of John's whole life makes him strong facing the cross. The rest of the Apostles flee from Golgotha. He, with the Mother of Christ, remains.

Don't forget that purity strengthens and invigorates your character.

145 The battle front in Madrid. A score of officers in noble and cheerful camaraderie. A song is heard, then another, and another...

That young lieutenant with the brown moustache only heard the first one:

> "I do not like
> divided hearts;
> and if I give mine,
> I give it whole."

"What resistance to give my heart whole!" And a prayer flowed forth in a calm, broad stream.

HEART

146   You give me the impression you are carrying your heart in your hands, as if you were offering goods for sale. Who wants it? If it doesn't appeal to anyone, you'll decide to give it to God.

Do you think that's how the saints acted?

147   Creatures for you? Creatures for God. If for you, let them be yours for his sake.

148   Why stoop to drink from the puddles of worldly consolations if you can satisfy your thirst with waters that spring up into life everlasting?

149   Detach yourself from creatures until you are stripped of them. For the devil, says Pope St Gregory, has nothing of his own in this world, and he goes into battle naked. If you are "clothed" when you fight with him, you'll soon be pulled down to the ground, because he will have something to grab on to.

150   It's as if your angel were saying to you, "You have your heart so full of human attachments"...Is that what you want your guardian to watch over?

151   Detachment. How hard it is! How I wish that I were fastened only by three nails and had no more feeling in my flesh than the cross!

152   Don't you sense that more peace and more union await you when you have corresponded to that extraordinary grace that requires complete detachment?

Struggle for him to please him, but strengthen your hope.

153 Go, generously and like a child ask him, "What are you going to give me when you ask 'this' of me?"

154 You're afraid of becoming distant and cold with everyone—you want so much to be detached!

Get rid of that fear. If you belong to Christ—completely to Christ—he will give you fire, light and warmth for all men.

155 Jesus is never satisfied "sharing". He wants all.

156 You don't want to submit yourself to the will of God...and instead you adapt yourself to the will of anybody and everybody.

157   Don't twist things around! If God gives himself to you, why are you so attached to creatures?

158   Now it's tears! It hurts, doesn't it? Of course, man! That's what it was meant to do.

159 Your heart weakens and you reach out for something on earth to support you. Good, but take care that what you grasp to stop you from falling doesn't become a dead weight that will drag you down, a chain that will enslave you.

160   Tell me, tell me: This...is it a friendship or a chain?

161   You squander your tenderness. And I tell you: "Charity toward your neighbor, yes: always." But listen closely, apostolic soul: that feeling which our Lord himself has placed in your heart is Christ's and Christ's alone.

Besides, when you opened one of the locks of your heart—which needs at least seven locks—isn't it true that more than once a cloud of doubt remained over your soul? And you asked yourself, worried in spite of the purity of your intentions, "Haven't I gone too far in my outward show of affection?"

162 Put your heart aside. Duty comes first. But, when fulfilling your duty, put your heart into it. It helps.

163 "If your right eye scandalizes you, pluck it out and cast it from you!" Poor heart...that's what scandalizes you!

Grasp it, hold it tight in your hands— and don't give it any consolation. And, when it asks for consolation, full of noble compassion say to it slowly, as if confiding, "My heart...heart on the cross, heart on the cross!"

164   How goes your heart?...Don't
be worried. The saints—who were perfectly ordinary, normal beings like you
and me—also felt those natural inclinations. And if they had not felt them, their
supernatural reaction of keeping their
heart—body and soul—for God, instead
of giving it to creatures, would have had
little merit.

That's why, once the way has been
seen, the weakness of the heart should be
no obstacle for a soul filled with determination and completely in Love.

165   You, who for an earthly love
have endured so many degradations, do
you really believe that you love Christ
when you are not willing to suffer—for
him!—that humiliation?

166   You write me: "Father, I have...
a 'toothache' in my heart." I won't laugh,

because I realize that you need a good dentist to make a few extractions.

If only you'd let him!...

167   "Oh, if only I had broken it off at the start!" you said to me. May you never have to repeat that belated exclamation.

168   "It made me laugh to hear you speak of the 'account' our Lord will demand of you. No, for you he will not be a judge—in the harsh sense of the word. He will simply be Jesus." These words, written by a holy bishop, have consoled more than one troubled heart and could very well console yours.

169   Suffering overwhelms you because you take it like a coward. Meet it bravely, with a christian spirit, and you will esteem it like a treasure.

170   How clear the way! How obvious the obstacles! What good weapons to overcome them! And yet, how many times you go astray and how many times you stumble! Isn't it true?

That fine thread—a chain, a chain forged of iron—which you and I know about and which you don't want to break: that is what draws you from the way and makes you stumble and even fall.

What are you waiting for? Cut it...and advance.

171   Love...is well worth any love!

MORTIFICATION

172   Unless you mortify yourself you'll never be a prayerful soul.

173   The appropriate word you left unsaid; the joke you didn't tell; the cheerful smile for those who bother you; that silence when you're unjustly accused; your kind conversation with people you find boring and tactless; the daily effort to overlook one irritating detail or another in those who live with you...this, with perseverance, is indeed solid interior mortification.

174   Don't say, "That person bothers me." Think: "That person sanctifies me."

175   No ideal becomes a reality without sacrifice. Deny yourself. It is so beautiful to be a victim!

176   How many times do you resolve to serve God in something and then have to content yourself—you are so weak—with offering him that frustrated feeling, the feeling of having failed to keep that easy resolution!

177   Don't miss a chance to "give in". It's hard—but how pleasing in the eyes of God!

178   Whenever you see a poor, wooden cross, alone, uncared-for, worthless...and without a corpus, don't forget that that cross is *your* cross—the everyday hidden cross, unattractive and unconsoling—the cross that is waiting for the corpus it lacks: and that corpus must be you.

179 Choose mortifications that don't mortify others.

180 Where there is no mortification, there is no virtue.

181 Interior mortification. I don't believe in your interior mortification if I see that you despise mortification of the senses—that you don't practice it.

182 In our poor present life, let us drink to the last drop from the chalice of pain. What does it matter to suffer for ten, twenty, fifty years, if afterwards there is heaven forever, forever...forever!

And above all—even better than for the sake of the reward, *propter retributionem*—what does suffering matter if we accept it to console, to please God our Lord, with a spirit of reparation, united with him on his cross—in a word, if we suffer for Love?...

183   The eyes! Through them much wickedness enters into the soul. How many experiences like David's!

If you guard your eyes, you'll be assured of guarding your heart.

184   Why should you look around you, if you carry "your world" within you?

185   The world admires only the spectacular sacrifice, because it does not realize the value of the sacrifice that is hidden and silent.

186   We must give ourselves in everything, we must deny ourselves in everything. Our sacrifice must be a holocaust.

187   Paradox: To live one must die.

188   Remember that the heart is a traitor. Keep it locked with seven bolts.

189 Everything that doesn't lead you to God is an obstacle. Tear it out and cast it far from you.

190 A soul whose immediate superior was bad tempered and irritable was moved by God to say, "Thank you, my God, for this truly divine treasure. Where would I find another to repay each kindness with a kick?"

191 Conquer yourself each day from the very first moment, getting up on the dot, at a set time, without granting a single minute to laziness.

If, with the help of God, you conquer yourself in that moment, you'll have accomplished a great deal for the rest of the day.

It's so discouraging to find yourself beaten in the first skirmish!

192 You always come out beaten. Resolve, each time, to work for the salvation of a particular soul, or his sanctification, or his vocation to the apostolate. If you do so, I'll be sure of your victory.

193   Don't be "namby pamby"! That's not the way I want you. It's time you get rid of that peculiar pity that you feel for yourself.

194   I'm going to tell you which are man's treasures on earth so you won't slight them: hunger, thirst, heat, cold, pain, dishonor, poverty, loneliness, betrayal, slander, prison...

195   It is true, whoever said it, that the soul and the body are two enemies that cannot be separated, and two friends that cannot get along.

196   The body must be given a little less than it needs. Otherwise it will turn traitor.

197 If they have witnessed your weaknesses and faults, does it matter if they witness your penance?

198 These are the savory fruits of the mortified soul: tolerance and understanding toward the defects of others; intolerance toward his own.

199 If the grain of wheat does not die, it remains unfruitful. Don't you want to be a grain of wheat, to die through mortification, and to yield stalks rich in grain? May Jesus bless your wheatfield!

200 You don't conquer yourself, you aren't mortified, because you are proud. You lead a life of penance? Remember: pride can exist with penance.

Furthermore: Your sorrow, after your falls, after your failures in generosity, is it really sorrow or is it the frustration of seeing yourself so small and weak?

How far you are from Jesus if you are not humble...even if new roses blossom every day from your disciplines!

201   What a taste of gall and vinegar, or ash and bitterness! What a dry mouth, coated and cracked! Yet that physical feeling is nothing compared with the bad taste in your soul.

The truth is that "more is being asked of you" and you can't bring yourself to give it. Humble yourself! Would that bitter taste still remain in your flesh and in your spirit if you did all that you could?

202   You're going to punish yourself voluntarily for your weakness and your lack of generosity? Good. But let it be a reasonable penance imposed, as it were, on an enemy who is at the same time your brother.

203   The happiness of us poor men, even when it has supernatural motives, always leaves a bitter aftertaste. What did you expect? Here on earth, suffering is the salt of our life.

204   Many who would let themselves be nailed to a cross before the astonished gaze of thousands of spectators, won't bear the pinpricks of each day with a christian spirit!

But think, which is the more heroic?

205   We were reading—you and I— the heroically ordinary life of that man of God. And we saw him struggle whole months and years (what an "accounting" he kept in his particular examination of conscience!); one day at breakfast he would win, the next day he'd lose..."I didn't take butter...I did take butter!" he would jot down.

May we too—you and I—live our...
"drama" of the butter.

206   The heroic minute. It's time to
get up, on the dot! Without hesitation, a
supernatural thought and...up! The heroic
minute; here you have a mortification that
strengthens your will and does not weaken
your body.

207   Give thanks, as for a very
special favor, for that holy abhorrence that
you feel toward yourself.

PENANCE

208   Blessed be pain. Loved be pain. Sanctified be pain...Glorified be pain!

209   A whole program for a good course in the "subject" of suffering has been given to us by the Apostle: *"spe gaudentes"*—"rejoicing in hope," *"in tribulatione patientes"*—"patient in tribulation," *"orationi instantes"*—"persevering in prayer."

210   Atonement: this is the path that leads to life.

211   Do penance: bury your negligences, offenses and sins in the deep pit dug by your humility. Thus does the farmer bury rotten fruit, dead twigs and fallen leaves at the foot of the tree that bore them. And what was unfruitful, even harmful, makes a real contribution to a new fertility.

Learn to draw from your falls a new impulse: from death, life.

212   That Christ you see is not Jesus. At best it is only the pitiful image that your blurred eyes are able to form...

Purify yourself. Make your sight cleaner with humility and penance. Then the pure light of love will not fail you. And you will have perfect vision. The image you see will really be his: Jesus himself.

213   Jesus suffers to carry out the will of the Father. And you, who also want to carry out the most holy will of God, following the steps of the Master, can you complain if you meet suffering on your way?

214 Say to your body: "I would rather keep you in slavery than be myself your slave."

215 What great fear people have of atonement! If what they do to please the world were done with purified intention for God, what saints many would be!

216 You are weeping? Don't be ashamed. Weep! Yes, for men also weep like you when they are alone and before God. At night, says King David, I bathe my bed with tears.

With those burning and manly tears, you can purify your past and supernaturalize your present life.

217 I want you to be happy on earth. But you won't be if you don't get rid of that fear of suffering. For as long as we are "wayfarers", it is precisely in suffering that our happiness lies.

218   How beautiful it is to give up this life for *the* life!

219   If you realize that those sufferings—physical or spiritual—are purification and merit, bless them.

220   "God give you health, brother." Doesn't this wish for physical well-being, with which some beggars demand or acknowledge alms, produce a bad taste in your mouth?

221   If we are generous in our voluntary atonement, Jesus will fill us with grace so that we can love the trials he sends us.

222   May your will exact from your senses—by means of atonement—what the other faculties deny your will in prayer.

223 How little penance is worth without constant mortification!

224 You are afraid of penance?...Of penance, which will help you to obtain life everlasting. Yet, do you see how men submit themselves to the thousand tortures of a painful surgical operation in order to preserve this poor present life?

225 Your worst enemy is yourself.

226 Treat your body with charity, but with no more charity than you would show toward a treacherous enemy.

227 If you realize that your body is your enemy, and an enemy of God's glory since it is enemy of your sanctification, why do you treat it so softly?

228 "Have a good time," they said as usual. And the comment of a soul very close to God was, "What a limited wish!"

229   With you, Jesus, how joyful is pain and how bright is darkness!

230   You are suffering! Listen: "his" heart is no smaller than ours. You are suffering? That's for the best.

231   A strict fast is a penance most pleasing to God. But with one thing and another, we've all grown lax. There is no objection—on the contrary!—if, with your director's approval, you fast frequently.

232   Motives for penance? Atonement, reparation, petition, thanksgiving; as a means of progress—for you, for me, for all the rest, for your family, for your country, for the Church...And a thousand motives more.

233   Don't perform more penance than your director allows.

234   How we ennoble suffering by giving it its due place (atonement) in the economy of the spirit!

EXAMINATION
OF CONSCIENCE

235   Examination of conscience. A daily task. Bookkeeping—never neglected by anyone in business.

And is there any business worth more than that of eternal life?

236   At the time of your examination beware of the devil that ties your tongue.

237   Examine yourself: slowly, with courage. Isn't it true that your bad temper and your sadness—both without cause, without apparent cause—are due to your lack of determination in breaking the subtle but real snares laid for you—cunningly and attractively—by your concupiscence?

238 The general examination is a weapon of defense. The particular, of attack. The first is the shield. The second, the sword.

239 A glance at the past. To bewail it? No: that is useless. To learn: that is fruitful.

240 Ask for light. Insist on it...until the root is laid bare and you can get at it with your battle-axe: the particular examination.

241 In your particular examination you have to go straight toward the acquisition of a definite virtue or toward the rooting out of the defect which is dominating you.

242   How much, as a Christian, I owe God! My lack of correspondence to his grace in the face of that debt has made me weep with sorrow—the sorrow of love. "*Mea culpa!*"—"Through my fault!"

It is good that you acknowledge your debts, but don't forget how they are paid: with tears...and with works.

243   "*Qui fidelis est in minimo et in maiori fidelis est*"—"He who is faithful in a very little thing is faithful also in much." Words from St Luke that show you—examine yourself—why you have so often gone astray.

244   Wake up! Listen to what the Holy Spirit is saying to you: "*Si inimicus meus maledixisset mihi, sustinuissem utique*"—"If my enemy had reviled me I would verily have borne with it." But you..."*tu vero homo unanimis, dux meus, et notus meus, qui simul mecum dulces*

capiebas cibos"—"you, my friend, my
apostle, who sit at my table and take sweet
food with me!"

245　　During a retreat your examination should be much deeper and much
longer than that usual nightly moment.
Otherwise you miss a great chance to
straighten things out.

246　　Always end your examination
with an act of love—sorrow of love: for
yourself, for all the sins of mankind. And
consider the fatherly care of God in re-
moving obstacles in your way lest you
should stumble.

RESOLUTIONS

247   Be specific. Don't let your resolutions be like fireworks that sparkle for an instant, only to leave as bitter reality a blackened, useless butt that is disgustedly thrown away.

248   You are so young! You seem to me like a ship beginning its voyage. That present slight deviation will in the end keep you from port, unless you correct it now.

249   Make few resolutions. Make specific resolutions. And fulfill them with the help of God.

250   I listened in silence as you said to me, "Yes, I want to be a saint"—although generally I have little respect for such a broad and vague assertion.

251   "Tomorrow!" Sometimes it is prudence; many times it is the adverb of the defeated.

252   Make this firm and determined resolution: to recall, when you receive honors and praise, everything that brings you shame and embarrassment.

The shame and embarrassment are yours; the praise and the glory are God's.

253   Conduct yourself well "now," without looking back on "yesterday" which is really gone, and without worrying about "tomorrow," which for you may never come.

254 Now! Return to your noble life now. Don't let yourself be fooled. "Now" is not too soon...nor too late.

255 Do you want me to tell you everything I think about "your way"?

Well, it's like this. If you really correspond to his call, you'll work for Christ like the best. If you become a man of prayer, you'll be given that correspondence I mentioned, and hungry for sacrifice, you'll seek the hardest tasks...

And you'll be happy here, and most happy hereafter—in the life.

256 That wound is painful. But it is well on its way to being healed. Be firm in your resolutions, and the pain will soon turn into joy and peace.

257 You drag along like a sandbag. You don't do your share. No wonder you are beginning to feel the first symptoms of lukewarmness. Wake up!

SCRUPLES

258   Get rid of those scruples that deprive you of peace. What robs you of your peace of soul cannot come from God.

When God comes to you, you will realize the truth of those greetings: My peace I give to you...My peace I leave with you...My peace be with you...And this peace you will feel even in the midst of tribulation.

259   Still those scruples! Talk simply and clearly with your director.

Obey...and don't belittle the most loving heart of our Lord.

260   Sadness, depression. I'm not surprised: it's the cloud of dust raised by your fall. But...enough of it! Can't you see that the cloud has been borne far away by the breath of grace?

Moreover, your sadness—if you don't reject it—could very well be the cloak of your pride. Did you really think yourself perfect and sinless?

261   I forbid you to think any more about it. Instead, bless God, who has given life back to your soul.

262   Don't think any more about your fall. Besides overwhelming and crushing you under its weight, that recollection may easily be an occasion of future temptation.

Christ has forgiven you! Forget the "old man"—your former self.

263 Don't be disheartened. I have seen you struggle. Today's defeat is training for the final victory.

264 You've done well, even though you have fallen so low. You've done well, because you humbled yourself, because you straightened yourself out, because you filled yourself with hope—and that hope brought you back again to his Love.

Don't look so amazed: you've done well! You rose up from the ground. "*Surge*"—"Arise"—cried anew the mighty voice—"*et ambula*"—"and walk!" Now—to work.

PRESENCE OF GOD

265   Children. How they seek to behave worthily in the presence of their fathers!

And the children of kings, in the presence of their father, the king, how they seek to uphold the royal dignity!

And you...Don't you realize that you are always in the presence of the great king, God, your Father?

266   Never make a decision without stopping to consider the matter in the presence of God.

267   It's necessary to be convinced that God is always near us. Too often we live as though our Lord were somewhere far off—where the stars shine. We fail to realize that he is also by our side—always.

For he is a loving Father. He loves each one of us more than all the mothers in the world can love their children, helping us and inspiring us, blessing...and forgiving.

How often we've erased the frowns from our parents' brows, telling them after some prank, "I won't do it again!" Maybe that same day we fall again...And our father, with feigned harshness in his voice and a serious face, reproves us, while at the same time his heart is softened because he knows our weakness: "Poor boy," he thinks, "How hard he tries to behave well!"

We have to be completely convinced, realizing it to the full, that our Lord, who is close to us and in heaven, is a Father, and very much *our* Father.

268   Make it a habit to raise your heart to God, in acts of thanksgiving, many times a day. Because he gives you this and that...Because someone has despised you...Because you don't have what you need, or because you do have it.

And because he made his Mother, who is also your Mother, so beautiful. Because he created the sun and the moon and this animal or that plant. Because he made that man eloquent and you he left slow of speech...

Thank him for everything, because everything is good.

269 Don't be so blind or so thoughtless that you fail to "go into" each tabernacle when you glimpse the walls or the steeple of each house of our Lord. He is waiting for you.

Don't be so blind or so thoughtless that you fail to say at least an ejaculation to Mary Immaculate, whenever you go past a place where you know Christ is being offended.

270   As you make your usual way through the city streets, aren't you happy when you discover another tabernacle?

271   Said a prayerful soul: In intentions, may Jesus be our end; in affections, our love; in speech, our theme; in actions, our model.

272   Make use of those holy "human devices" I've recommended to keep you from losing the presence of God: ejaculations, acts of love and reparation, spiritual communions, "glances" at a picture of our Lady.

273   Alone! You are *not* alone. We are keeping you close company from afar. Besides abiding in your soul in grace is the Holy Spirit—God with you!—giving a supernatural tone to all your thoughts, desires and works.

274 "Father," said that big fellow, a good student at the Central* (I wonder what has become of him), "I was thinking of what you told me—that I'm a son of God!—and I found myself walking along the street, head up, chin out, and a feeling of pride inside...a son of God!"

With sure conscience I advised him to foster that "pride."

275 I don't doubt your good intentions. I know you act in the presence of God. But—and there is a "but"!—your actions are witnessed or may be witnessed by men who judge by human standards... And you must set a good example for them.

276 If you accustom yourself, at least once a week, to seek union with

---

*The Central: how the University of Madrid was called at the time *The Way* was written.

Mary in order to go to Jesus, you will have more presence of God.

277   You ask me, "Why that wooden cross?" And I quote from a letter: "As I raise my eyes from the microscope, my sight comes to rest on the cross—black and empty. That cross without a corpus is a symbol; it has a meaning others won't see. And I, tired out and on the point of abandoning my work, once again bring my eyes close to the lens and continue. For that lonely cross is calling for a pair of shoulders to bear it."

278   Live in the presence of God and you will have supernatural life.

SUPERNATURAL LIFE

279   People see only the flat surface. Their vision is two-dimensional and fixed to the ground.

When you live a supernatural life, God will give you the third-dimension: height, and with it, perspective, weight and volume.

280   If you lose the supernatural meaning of your life, your charity will be philanthropy; your purity, decency; your mortification, stupidity; your discipline, a lash; and all your works, fruitless.

281   Silence is the doorkeeper of the interior life.

282   Paradox: Sanctity is more attainable than learning, but it is easier to be a scholar than to be a saint.

283   A little diversion! You've got to have a change! So you open your eyes wide to let in images of things, or you squint because you're nearsighted!

Close them altogether! Have interior life, and you'll see the wonders of a better world, a new world with undreamed-of color and perspective...and you'll draw close to God. You'll feel your weaknesses; and you'll become more Godlike... with a godliness that will make you more of a brother to your fellowmen by bringing you closer to your Father.

284   Aspiration: that I be good, and everyone else be better than I!

285   Conversion is a matter of a moment. Sanctification is the work of a lifetime.

286 There is nothing better in the world than to be in the grace of God.

287 Purity of intention: You'll have it always, if you seek ever and in all things to please only God.

288 Enter into the wounds of Christ crucified. There you will learn to guard your senses, you will have interior life, and you will continually offer to the Father the sufferings of our Lord and those of Mary, in payment of your debts and the debts of all men.

289 Your holy impatience to serve God doesn't displease him. But it will be barren if it is not accompanied by an effective improvement in your daily conduct.

290 To reform. Every day a little. This has to be your constant task if you really want to become a saint.

291   You have the obligation to sanctify yourself. Yes, even you. Who thinks this is the exclusive concern of priests and religious?

To everyone, without exception, our Lord said: "Be perfect, as my heavenly Father is perfect."

292   Your interior life has to be just that: to begin...and to begin again.

293   In your interior life, have you taken the time to consider the beauty of *serving* with actual willingness?

294   The plants were hidden under the snow. And the farmer, the owner of the land, remarked with satisfaction: "Now they're growing on the inside."

I thought of you, of your forced inactivity...Tell me, are you also growing on the inside?

295 If you are not master of yourself—even if you're powerful—acting the master is to me something laughable and to be pitied.

296 It is hard to read in the holy Gospel that question of Pilate's: "Whom do you wish that I release to you, Barabbas or Jesus, who is called the Christ?" But it is more painful to hear the answer: "Barabbas!"

And it is more terrible still when I realize that very often—when I have wandered away—I, too, have said, "Barabbas!" And I've added, "Christ?... *Crucifige eum!*—Crucify him!"

297 All that worries you for the moment is only of passing importance. What is of absolute importance is that you be happy...that you be saved!

298 New lights! What joy you feel that God has let you find "it's really true!"

Take advantage of the occasion. It is the moment to break into a hymn of thanksgiving. And it is also the moment to dust the odd corners of your soul, to get out of your rut, to put more of the supernatural into your work, to avoid a possible scandal to your neighbor.

In a word: let your gratitude be shown in some specific resolution.

299   Christ died for you. You...what should you do for Christ?

300   Your personal experience—that dejection, that restlessness, that bitterness—brings to life the truth of those words of Jesus: No one can serve two masters!

MORE ABOUT
INTERIOR LIFE

301   I'll tell you a secret, an open secret: these world crises are crises of saints.

God wants a handful of men "of his own" in every human activity. Then... *"pax Christi in regno Christi"*—"the peace of Christ in the kingdom of Christ."

302   Your crucifix: As a Christian you should always carry a crucifix with you. Place it on your desk. Kiss it before you go to bed and when you wake up. And when your poor body rebels against your soul, kiss your crucifix!

303   Don't be afraid to call our Lord by his name—Jesus—and to tell him that you love him.

304   Each day try to find a few minutes of that blessed solitude you need so much to keep your interior life going.

305   You wrote me: "Simplicity is the salt of perfection. And that's what I lack. I want to acquire it, with his help and with yours."

You'll lack neither his help nor mine. Use the means.

306   "The life of man upon earth is warfare." So said Job many centuries ago.

There are still some easygoing individuals unaware of this fact.

307   That supernatural way of conducting yourself is real military strategy. You carry on the war—the daily battles of your interior life—in positions far from the main walls of your fortress.

And the enemy comes to meet you there: in your small mortification, in your daily prayer, in your orderly work, in your plan of life. And only with difficulty does he get close to the otherwise easily-scaled battlements of your citadel. And if he does, he arrives exhausted.

308   You write and I quote: "My joy and my peace. I can never have real happiness if I have no peace. And what is peace? Peace is something intimately associated with war. Peace is the result of victory. Peace demands of me a constant struggle. Without that struggle, I'll never be able to have peace."

309   Consider what depths of mercy lie in the justice of God! For, according to human justice, he who pleads guilty is punished, but in the divine court, he is pardoned.

Blessed be the holy sacrament of penance!

310 *"Induimini dominum Iesum Christum"*—"Put on the Lord Jesus Christ," says St Paul to the Romans. It is in the sacrament of penance that you and I put on Jesus Christ and his merits.

311 War! "War has a supernatural end that the world is unaware of," you tell me, "because war has been for us..."

War is the greatest obstacle to the easy way. But in the end we have to love it, as the religious should love his disciplines.

312 The power of your name, Lord! As a heading to my letter I had written, as I usually do, "May Jesus watch over you."

Then came the reply: "That 'May Jesus watch over you!' of your letter has already helped me out of more than one tight corner. May he also watch over all of you."

313   "Now that our Lord is helping me with his usual generosity, I will try to correspond by bettering my ways." So you told me. And I had nothing to add.

314   I wrote to you and said: "I'm relying on you. You'll see what we can do...!" What could we do, except rely on him!

315   A missionary. You dream of being a missionary. You vibrate like a Xavier, longing to conquer an empire for Christ—Japan, China, India, Russia; the peoples of North Europe, or of America, or Africa, or Australia!

Foster that fire in your heart, that hunger for souls. But don't forget that you're more of a missionary obeying. Geographically far away from those apostolic fields, you work both here and there. Don't you feel your arm tired—like Xavier's!—after administering baptism to so many?

316   You tell me: "Yes, I want to!" Good. But do you "want to" as a miser wants his gold, as a mother wants her child, as a worldling wants honors, or as a poor sensualist wants his pleasure?

No? Then you don't "want to!"

317   What zeal men put into their earthly affairs! Dreaming of honors, striving for riches, bent on sensuality! Men and women, rich and poor, old and middle-aged and young and even children: all of them alike.

When you and I put the same zeal into the affairs of our souls, then we'll have a living and working faith. And there will be no obstacle that we cannot overcome in our apostolic works.

318   To you who like sports, the words of the Apostle should really make sense: "*Nescitis quod ii qui in stadio currunt omnes quidem currunt, sed unus*

*accipit bravium? Sic currite ut compre-
hendatis"*—"Do you not know that those
who run in the race, all indeed run, but one
receives the prize? So run as to obtain it."

319   Withdraw into yourself. Seek
God within you and listen to him.

320   Foster those noble thoughts,
those incipient holy desires...A single
spark can start a conflagration.

321   Apostolic soul, that intimacy
between Jesus and you—so close to him
for so many years! Doesn't it mean anything to you?

322   It's true that I always call our
tabernacle Bethany. Become a friend of
the Master's friends—Lazarus, Martha,
Mary—and then you will ask me no more
why I call our tabernacle Bethany.

323   You know that there are "counsels of the Gospel". To follow them is a refinement of love.

They say it is the way of the few. At times I feel that it could be the way of many.

324   *"Quia hic homo coepit aedificare et non potuit consummare!"*—"This man began to build and was not able to finish!" A sad commentary which need never be made about you, if you don't wish it to be. For you possess everything necessary to crown the edifice of your sanctification: the grace of God and your own will.

LUKEWARMNESS

325   Fight against the softness that makes you lazy and careless in your spiritual life. Remember that it might well be the beginning of tepidity...and, in the words of the Scripture, God will vomit out the lukewarm.

326   It hurts me to see you place yourself in danger of tepidity when you don't go straight toward perfection within your state in life.

Say with me: I don't want to be lukewarm! *"Confige timore tuo carnes meas!"*—"Pierce my flesh with your fear!" Grant me, my God, a filial fear that will stir me up!

327   I already know that you avoid mortal sins. You want to be saved! But you are not worried about that constant and deliberate falling into venial sins, even though in each case you feel God's call to conquer yourself.

It is your lukewarmness that makes you so badly disposed.

328   What little love for God you have when you give in without a fight because it's not a grave sin!

329   Venial sins do great harm to the soul. That's why our Lord says in the *Canticle of Canticles*: "*capite nobis vulpes parvulas, quae demoliuntur vineas*"— "catch the little foxes that destroy the vines."

330   How sad you make me feel when you are not sorry for your venial sins! For, until you are, you cannot begin to have true interior life.

331 You are tepid if you carry out listlessly and reluctantly those things that have to do with our Lord; if deliberately or "shrewdly" you look for some way of lessening your duties; if you think only of yourself and of your comfort; if your conversation is idle and vain; if you don't abhor venial sin; if you act from human motives.

STUDY

332   There is no excuse for those who could be scholars and are not.

333   Study. Obedience. *Non multa, sed multum*—not many things, but well.

334   You pray, you mortify yourself, you labor at a thousand apostolic activities...but you don't study. You are useless then, unless you change your ways.

Study—any professional development—is a serious obligation for us.

335   An hour of study, for a modern apostle, is an hour of prayer.

336 If you are to serve God with your mind, to study is a grave obligation for you.

337 You frequent the sacraments, you pray, you are chaste, but you don't study. Don't tell me you're good; you're only "goodish."

338 Formerly, when human knowledge—science—was very limited, it seemed quite feasible for a single scholar to defend and vindicate our holy faith.

Today, with the extension and the intensity of modern science, the apologists have to divide the work among themselves, if they wish to defend the Church scientifically in all fields.

You...cannot shirk this responsibility.

339 Books. Don't buy them without advice from a Catholic who has real knowledge and discernment. It's so easy to buy something useless or harmful.

How often a man thinks he is carrying a book under his arm, and it turns out to be a load of trash!

340 Study. Study in earnest. If you are to be salt and light, you need knowledge, capability.

Or do you imagine that an idle and lazy life will entitle you to receive infused knowledge?

341 It's good for you to put such determination into your study, as long as you put the same determination into acquiring interior life.

342 Don't forget that before teaching one must act. "*Coepit facere et docere*," the holy Scripture says of Jesus Christ: "He began to do and to teach."

First, action: so that you and I may learn.

343   Work! When you are engrossed in professional work, the life of your soul will improve, and you'll become more of a man for you'll get rid of that "carping spirit" that consumes you.

344   Teacher: your undeniable keenness to know and practise the best methods of helping your students acquire earthly knowledge is good. But be equally keen to know and practise christian asceticism, which is the only method of helping them and yourself to be better.

345   Culture, culture! Good! Don't let anyone get ahead of us in striving for it and possessing it.

But remember that culture is a means, not an end.

346   Student: form in yourself a solid and active piety; be outstanding in study; have strong desires for a professional apostolate. And with that vigor in your religious and scientific training, I promise you rapid and far-reaching developments.

347 You worry only about building up your culture. But what you really need to build up is your soul. Then you will work as you should—for Christ.

In order that he may reign in the world, it is necessary to have people of prestige who with their eyes fixed on heaven, dedicate themselves to all human activities, and through those activities exercise quietly—and effectively—an apostolate of a professional character.

348 Your indolence, your carelessness, your laziness are really cowardice and sloth—so your conscience continually tells—but they are not "the way".

349 Don't be upset when you state an orthodox opinion and the malice of whoever heard you caused him to be scandalized. For his scandal is pharisaical.

350   In addition to being a good Christian, it's not enough to be a scholar. If you don't correct your rudeness, if you make your zeal and your knowledge incompatible with good manners, I don't see how you can ever become a saint. And, even if you are a scholar—in spite of being a scholar—you should be tied to a stall, like a mule.

351   With that self-satisfied air you're becoming an unbearable and repulsive character. You're making a fool of yourself, and what is worse, you're diminishing the effect of your work as an apostle.

Don't forget that even the mediocre can sin by being too scholarly.

352   Your very inexperience leads you to presumption, vanity and to all that

you imagine gives you an air of importance.

Correct yourself, please! Foolish and
all, you may come to occupy a post of
responsibility (it's happened more than
once), and if you're not convinced of your
lack of ability, you will refuse to listen to
those who have the gift of counsel. And
it's frightening to think of the harm your
mismanagement will do.

353   Nonsectarianism. Neutrality.
Those old myths that always try to seem
new.

Have you ever bothered to think how
absurd it is to leave one's catholicism
aside on entering a university, or a professional association, or a scholarly meeting,
or Congress, as if you were checking your
hat at the door?

354   Make good use of your time.
Don't forget the fig tree cursed by our

Lord. And it was doing something: sprouting leaves. Like you...

Don't tell me you have excuses. It availed the fig tree little, relates the evangelist, that it was not the season for figs when our Lord came to it to look for them.

And barren it remained forever.

355 People engaged in worldly business say that time is money. That means little to me. For us who are engaged in the business of souls, time is glory!

356 I don't understand how you can call yourself a Christian and lead such an idle, useless life. Have you forgotten Christ's life of toil?

357 "All the sins," so you said, "seem to be waiting for the first idle moment. Really, idleness itself must be a sin!"

Whoever gives himself to work for Christ cannot expect to have a free moment, for even to rest is not to do nothing: it is to relax with activities that require less effort.

358   To be idle is something inconceivable in a man who has apostolic spirit.

359   Add a supernatural motive to your ordinary professional work and you will have sanctified it.

FORMING THE SPIRIT

360   How frankly you laughed when I advised you to put your youthful years under the protection of St Raphael, "so that he'll lead you, as he did young Tobias, to a holy marriage, with a girl who is good and pretty—and rich," I added jokingly.

And then how thoughtful you became, when I went on to advise you to put yourself also under the patronage of that youthful apostle John, in case God were to ask more of you.

361   For you who complain to yourself that they treat you harshly and who feel the contrast between this harshness and the conduct of those of your own blood, I copy these lines from the letter of an army doctor:

"Toward the sick there can be the cold and efficient attitude of an honest doctor, which is objective and useful to the patient, or the weeping tenderness of a family. What would happen at a first-aid station during a battle, when the stream of wounded begins to pour in, if around each stretcher there stood a family? One might as well go over to the enemy."

362 I have no need of miracles. There are more than enough in the Scriptures. But I do need the fulfillment of your duty, your correspondence to grace.

363 You're disheartened, crestfallen. Men have just taught you a lesson! They thought you didn't really need their help and so they made you plenty of empty promises. The possibility that they might have to help you with hard cash—just a few pennies—turned their friendship into indifference.

Trust only in God and those united with you through him.

364   Ah, if you would only resolve to serve God *seriously*, with the same earnestness that you put into serving your ambitions, your vanities, your sensuality...

365   If you feel an impulse to be a leader, this should be your aim: to be the last among your brothers and the first among all others.

366   Let's see: do you feel slighted because so-and-so enjoys more confidence with certain persons he knew before or to whom he feels more attracted by temperament, profession, or character?

All right, but among your own, carefully avoid even the appearance of any particularly close friendship.

367   The choicest morsel, if eaten by a pig, turns—to put it bluntly—into pig's meat!

Let us be angels, so as to dignify the ideas we assimilate.

Let us at least be men and convert our food into strong, fine muscles or perhaps into a powerful brain, capable of understanding and adoring God.

But, let us not be beasts, like so many, so very many!

368   You're bored? That's because you keep your senses awake and your soul asleep.

369   The charity of Jesus Christ will often lead you to make concessions—a noble yielding. And the charity of Jesus Christ will often lead you to stand fast. That too is very noble.

370   If you're not bad, and yet you seem to be, then you're a fool. And that foolishness—a cause of scandal—is even worse than being bad.

371 When you see people of doubtful professional reputation acting as leaders at public activities of a religious nature, don't you feel the urge to whisper in their ears: "Please, would you mind being just a little less Catholic!"

372 If you have an official position, you have certain rights and also certain duties which go with it.

You stray from your apostolic way if the occasion—or the excuse—of a work of zeal makes you leave the duties of your office unfulfilled. For you will lose your professional prestige, which is exactly your "bait" as a fisher of men.

373 I like your apostolic motto: "Work without resting."

374   Why that rushing around? Don't tell me it's activity: It's confusion!

375   Dissipation. You slake your senses and faculties at whatever puddle you meet on the way. And then you experience the results: unsettled purpose, scattered attention, deadened will, aroused concupiscence.

Subject yourself again seriously to a plan that will make you lead a christian life. Otherwise you'll never do anything worthwhile.

376   "Environment is such an influence," you've told me. And I have had to answer: No doubt. That's why you have to be formed in such a way that you can carry your own environment about with you in a natural manner, and so give your own tone to the society in which you live.

And then, when you've acquired this spirit, I'm sure you'll tell me with all the amazement of the early disciples as they contemplated the first fruits of the miracles performed by their hands in Christ's name: "How great is our influence on our environment!"

377   And how shall I acquire "our formation" and how shall I keep "our spirit"? By being faithful to the specific "norms" that your director gave you, and explained to you, and made you love. Be faithful to them and you'll be an apostle.

378   Don't be a pessimist. Don't you realize that everything that happens or can happen is for the best?

Optimism will be a necessary consequence of your faith.

379   Naturalness. Let your christian spirit—your salt and your light—be manifested spontaneously, without anything

odd or foolish. Always carry with you
your spirit of simplicity.

380   "And in a pagan or in a worldly
atmosphere, when my life clashes with its
surroundings, won't my naturalness seem
artificial?" you ask me.

And I reply: Undoubtedly your life
will clash with theirs; and that contrast—
because you're confirming your faith with
works—is exactly the naturalness I ask of
you.

381   Don't worry if people say you
have too much *esprit de corps*. What do
they want? A delicate instrument that
breaks to pieces the moment it is grasped?

382   When I made you a present of
that *Life of Jesus*, I wrote in it this inscription: "May you seek Christ. May you find
Christ. May you love Christ."

These are three very distinct steps. Have you at least tried to live the first one?

383   If they see you weaken—you, the leader—it is no wonder their obedience wavers.

384   Confusion. I knew you were unsure of the rightness of your judgment. And, so that you might understand me, I wrote you: "The devil has a very ugly face, and since he's so smart he won't risk our seeing his horns. He never makes a direct attack. That's why he so often comes in the disguise of nobleness and even of spirituality!"

385   Our Lord says: "A new commandment I give you: that you love one another. By this shall all men know that you are my disciples."

And St Paul: "Bear each other's burdens, and thus you shall fulfill the law of Christ."

I have nothing to add.

386   Don't forget, my son, that for you there is but one evil on earth: sin. You must fear it and avoid it with the grace of God.

YOUR SANCTITY

387   The plane of the sanctity our Lord asks of us is determined by these three points: holy steadfastness, holy forcefulness and holy shamelessness.

388   Holy shamelessness is one thing, and worldly boldness quite another.

389   Holy shamelessness is characteristic of the life of childhood. A little child doesn't worry about anything. He makes no effort to hide his weaknesses, his natural weaknesses, even though everyone is watching him.

Shamelessness, carried to the supernatural life, suggests this train of reasoning: praise, contempt; admiration, scorn; honor, dishonor; health, illness; riches, poverty; beauty, ugliness...Well, all right, does it matter?

390   Laugh at ridicule. Scorn whatever may be said. See and feel God in yourself and in your surroundings. Thus you will soon acquire the holy shamelessness you need in order to live, paradoxically, with the refinement of a christian gentleman.

391   If you have holy shamelessness, you won't be bothered by the thought of what people have said or what they will say.

392   Convince yourself that ridicule does not exist for those who are doing what is best.

393 A man—a gentleman—ready to compromise would condemn Jesus to death again.

394 Compromising is a sure sign of not possessing the truth. When a man yields in matters of ideals, of honor or of faith, that man is without ideals, without honor, and without faith.

395 That man of God, an old campaigner, argued like this: So I won't yield an inch. And why should I, if I am convinced of the truth of my ideals? You, on the other hand, are very ready to compromise. Would you agree that two and two are three and a half? No? Not even for friendship's sake would you yield in such a little thing.

It's simply because, for the first time, you feel convinced that you possess the truth...and you've come over to my side!

396   Holy steadfastness is not intolerance.

397   Be steadfast in doctrine and in conduct, but pliant in manner: a powerful blacksmith's hammer wrapped in a quilted covering.

Be steadfast, but don't be obstinate.

398   Steadfastness is not simply intransigence: it is "holy intransigence".

Don't forget that there also exists a "holy forcefulness".

399   If, to save an earthly life, it is praiseworthy to use force to keep a man from committing suicide, are we not allowed to use the same coercion—"holy coercion"—in order to save the Lives (with a capital) of so many who are stupidly bent on killing their souls?

400   How many crimes are committed in the name of justice! If you were a dealer in guns and someone paid you for one so that he might use it to kill your mother, would you sell it to him? And yet, wasn't he ready to pay you a just price for it?

Professor, journalist, politician, diplomat: meditate.

401   God and daring! Daring is not imprudence. Daring is not recklessness.

402   Don't ask Jesus to forgive only your own faults: don't love him with *your* heart alone.

Console him for every offense that has been, is, and will be done to him. Love him with all the strength of all the hearts of all the men who have loved him most.

Be daring: tell him you are carried away with more love than Mary Magdalene, more than Teresa and little Therese, more carried away than Augustine and Dominic and Francis, more than Ignatius and Xavier.

403   Be more daring still, and whenever you need anything, mindful always of the *"Fiat"*—"Your will be done"—don't ask, tell him: "Jesus, I want this or that". For that's the way children ask.

404   You say you've failed! We *never* fail. You placed your confidence wholly in God. And you did not neglect any human means.

Convince yourself of this truth: your success—this time—was to fail. Give thanks to our Lord, and try again!

405   So you've failed? You—be convinced of it—can never fail.

You haven't failed; you've acquired experience. Forward!

406   That was a failure, a disaster, because you lost your spirit. You know well that as long as we act for supernatural motives, the outcome (victory? defeat? Bah!) has only one name: success.

407 Let's not confuse the rights of the office with personal rights. The former can never be renounced.

408 Sanctimony is to sanctity what "piosity" is to piety: its caricature.

409 Remember that even if your virtues seem saintly, they're worth nothing if they are not united to the ordinary christian virtues.

That would be like adorning yourself with splendid jewels over your underclothes.

410 May your virtue not be noisy.

411 Many false apostles, in spite of themselves, do good to the masses, to the people, through the very power of the doctrine of Jesus which they preach—even though they don't practise it.

But this good does not compensate for the enormous and very real harm they do by killing the souls of leaders, of apostles, who turn away in disgust from those who don't practise what they preach.

That's why such men and women, if they are not willing to live an upright life, should never push themselves forward as leaders.

412   May the fire of your love not be a will-ó-the-wisp, a vain fire, an illusion— an illusion of fire, which neither enkindles what it touches nor gives any heat.

413   The "*non serviam*"—"I will not serve"—of Satan has been too fruitful. Don't you feel the generous impulse to say every day, with desires for prayer and deeds, a *serviam*—"I will serve you, I will be faithful!"—surpassing in fruitfulness that cry of rebellion?

414   How pathetic: a "man of God" who has fallen away! But how much more pathetic: a "man of God" who is lukewarm and worldly!

415 Don't worry too much about what the world calls victories or defeats. How often the "victor" ends up defeated!

416 "*Sine me nihil potestis facere!*"—"Without me you can do nothing!" New light—new *splendor*—for my eyes, from the eternal light, the holy Gospel.

Now should I be surprised at all of "my" foolishness?

Let me put Jesus into everything that is mine; then there will be no foolishness in my conduct. And if I would speak correctly, I would talk no more of what is "mine", but of what is "ours".

LOVE OF GOD

417 The only real love is God's love!

418 The secret that ennobles the humblest things, even the most humiliating, is to love.

419 Children...the sick...As you write these words, don't you feel tempted to write them with capitals?

The reason is that in little children and in the sick a soul in love sees him!

420 How little a life is to offer to God!

421   A friend is a treasure. Well... you have a friend! For where your treasure is, there is your heart.

422   Jesus is your Friend—*the* friend —with a human heart, like yours, with most loving eyes that wept for Lazarus.

And as much as he loved Lazarus, he loves you...

423   My God, I love you, but...oh, teach me to love!

424   To punish for the sake of Love: this is the secret that raises to a supernatural plane any punishment imposed on those who deserve it.

For the love of God, who has been offended, let punishment serve as atonement. For the love of our neighbor, for the sake of God, may punishment never be revenge, but a healing medicine.

425   To realize that you love me so much, my God, and yet I haven't lost my mind!

426   In Christ we have every ideal: for he is King, he is Love, he is God.

427   Lord, may I have balance and measure in everything—except in Love.

428   If Love, even human love, gives so many consolations here, what will Love be in heaven?

429   Everything done for the sake of Love acquires greatness and beauty.

430   Jesus, may I be the last in everything...and the first in Love.

431　　Don't fear God's justice. It is no less admirable and no less lovable than his mercy. Both are proofs of his love.

432　　Consider what is most beautiful and most noble on earth, what pleases the mind and the other faculties, and what delights the flesh and the senses. Consider the world, and the other worlds that shine in the night—the whole universe.

And this, along with all the satisfied follies of the heart, is worth nothing, *is* nothing and less than nothing, compared with this God of mine!—of yours! Infinite treasure, most beautiful pearl...humbled, become a slave, reduced to nothingness in the form of a servant in the stable where he willed to be born...in Joseph's workshop, in his passion and in his ignominious death, and in the frenzy of Love—the blessed eucharist.

433   Live by Love and you will conquer always—even when you are defeated—in the Navas* and the Lepantos** of your interior life.

434   Let your heart overflow in effusions of love and gratitude as you consider how the grace of God saves you each day from the snares the enemy sets in your path.

435   *"Timor Domini sanctus"*— "The fear of the Lord is holy." This fear is a son's veneration for his Father—never a servile fear. For God, your Father, is not a tyrant.

---

*The Navas of Tolosa: famous battle that occurred in 1212 in southern Spain, won by the armies of the Christian kingdoms of the Iberian Peninsula over the Moslems of Andalusia and northern Africa.

**Lepanto: naval battle that took place in the Mediterranean Sea in 1571 between a Turkish and a Christian squadron. It was won by the Christian fleet.

436   Sorrow of love—because he is good; because he is your friend, who gave his life for you; because everything good you have is his, because you have offended him so much, ...because he has forgiven you. He! Forgiven *you*!

Weep, my son, with sorrow of love.

437   If one of my fellow men had died to save me from death...

God died. And I remain indifferent.

438   Mad! Yes, I saw you (in the bishop's chapel, you thought you were alone) as you left a kiss on each newly-consecrated chalice and paten, so that he might find it there when for the first time he would "come down" to those eucharistic vessels.

439   Don't forget that sorrow is the touchstone of Love.

CHARITY

440 When you have finished your work, do your brother's, helping him, for the sake of Christ, with such finesse and naturalness that no one—not even he—will realize that you are doing more than in justice you ought.

This, indeed, is virtue befitting a son of God!

441 You are hurt by your neighbor's lack of charity toward you. Think how God must be hurt by your lack of charity—of love—toward him!

442 Never think badly of anyone, not even if the words or conduct of the

person in question give you good grounds
for doing so.

443   Don't make negative criticism.
If you can't praise, say nothing.

444   Never speak badly of your
brother, not even when you have plenty of
reasons for doing so. Go first to the tabernacle, and then go to the priest, your
father, and also tell him what is bothering
you.

And to no one else.

445   Gossip is trash that soils and
hinders the apostolate. It goes against
charity, takes away strength, takes away
peace, and makes one lose his union with
God.

446   If you have so many defects,
why are you surprised to find defects in
others?

447   After seeing how many people waste their lives (without a break: gab, gab, gab—and with all the consequences!), I can better appreciate how necessary and lovable silence is.

And I can well understand, Lord, why you will make us account for every idle word.

448   Talking comes easier than doing. You who have that cutting tongue—like a hatchet—have you ever tried, by chance, to do *well* what others, according to your "authoritative" opinion, do less well?

449   This is what that really is: grumbling, gossiping, tale-bearing, scandal-mongering, back-biting. Or even slander? Or viciousness?

When those who are not supposed to sit in judgment do so, they very easily end up as gossiping old maids.

450   How the injustice of the "just" offends God, how it harms many souls—and how it can sanctify others!

451   Let us be slow to judge. Each one sees things from his own point of view and with his own mind, with all its limitations, through eyes that are often dimmed and clouded by passion.

Moreover, like so many of those modern artists, some people have an outlook which is so subjective and so unhealthy that they make a few random strokes and assure us that these represent our portrait, our conduct. Of what little worth are the judgments of men!

Don't judge without sifting your judgment in prayer.

452   Force yourself, if necessary, always to forgive those who offend you, from the very first moment. For the greatest injury or offense you can suffer from them is nothing compared to what God has forgiven you.

453 Back-biting? Then you are losing the right spirit, and if you don't learn to check your tongue, each word will be one more step toward the exit from that apostolic undertaking in which you work.

454 Don't judge without having heard both sides. Even persons who think themselves virtuous very easily forget this elementary rule of prudence.

455 Can you know what damage you do throwing stones with your eyes blindfolded?

Neither do you know—because you're blinded by thoughtlessness or passion— the harm you produce, at times very great, dropping uncharitable comments that to you seem trifling.

456   To criticize, to destroy, is not difficult; the clumsiest laborer knows how to drive his pick into the noble and finely-hewn stone of a cathedral.

To construct—that is what requires the skill of a master.

457   Who are you to judge the rightness of a superior's decision? Don't you see that he has more basis for judging than you? He has more experience; he has more upright, experienced and impartial advisers; and above all, he has more grace, a special grace, the grace of his state, which is the light and the powerful aid of God.

458   Those clashes with the world's selfishness will make you appreciate much more the fraternal charity of your brother-apostles.

459   Your charity is presumptuous. From afar, you attract; you have light.

From nearby, you repel; you lack warmth.
What a pity!

460   *"Frater qui adiuvatur a fratre
quasi civitas firma."*—"A brother who is
helped by his brother is like a strong city."

Think for a moment and make up your
mind to live that brotherhood I've always
recommended to you.

461   If I don't see you practice that
blessed brotherly spirit that I preach to you
constantly, I'll remind you of those loving
words of St John: *"Filioli mei, non dil-
igamus verbo neque lingua, sed opere et
veritate"*—"My dear children, let us love
not in word, neither with the tongue but in
deed and in truth."

462   The power of charity! If you
live that blessed brotherly spirit, your
mutual weakness will also be a support to
keep you upright in the fulfillment of

duty—just as in a house of cards, one card supports the other.

463   Charity consists not so much in giving as in understanding. That's why you should seek an excuse for your neighbor—there are always excuses—if yours is the duty to judge.

464   You know that that person's soul is in danger? From afar, with your life of union, you can give him effective help. Help him, then, and don't worry.

465   I think it is all right for you to feel concern for your brothers—there is no better proof of your mutual love. Take care, however, to keep your worries from degenerating into anxiety.

466   "Generally," you write me, "people are not too generous with their money. Plenty of talk, noisy enthusiasm, promises, plans. But at the moment of sacrifice, few come forward to lend a hand. And if they do, it has to be with trimmings attached—a dance, a raffle, a movie, a show—or an announcement and subscription-list in the newspapers."

It's a sad state of affairs, but it has its exceptions. May you, too, be one of those who give alms without letting their left hand know what their right hand is doing.

467   Books. I put my hand out, like one of Christ's beggars, and I asked for books—books that are nourishment for the Roman, Catholic, and apostolic minds of many university students.

I put my hand out, like one of Christ's beggars, and each time had it brushed aside!

Why can't people understand, Jesus, the profound christian charity of this alms, more effective than a gift of the finest bread?

468   You were exceedingly naive. How few really practise charity! Being charitable doesn't mean giving away old clothes or copper pennies...And you tell me your tale of woe and disillusionment.

Only one idea occurs to me: let us—you and I—give and give ourselves unstintingly. And we'll keep those who come in contact with us from going through the same sad experience.

469   "Greet all the saints. All the saints send you greetings. To all the saints who are at Ephesus. To all the saints in Christ Jesus who are at Philippi." What a moving name—saints!—the early Christians used to address one another!

Learn how to treat your brothers.

THE MEANS

470 The means? They're the same as those of Peter and Paul, of Dominic and Francis, of Ignatius and Xavier: the cross and the Gospel.

Do they seem little to you, perhaps?

471 In apostolic undertakings it's very good—it's a duty—to consider what means the world has to offer you (2 + 2 = 4). But don't forget—ever—that your calculations must fortunately include another term: God + 2 + 2...

472 Serve your God straightforwardly; be faithful to him, and don't worry about anything else. For it's a great truth that if you "seek first the kingdom of God and his justice, all other things"—material things, the means—"will be given you besides". He will provide them for you.

473   Cast away that despair produced by the realization of your weakness. It's true: financially you are a zero, and socially another zero, and another in virtues, and another in talent...

But to the left of these zeros is Christ... And what an immeasurable figure it turns out to be!

474   So you are a nobody. And others have done wonders—are still doing them—through organization, through the press, through promotion. And they have all the means, while you have none. Well, then, just remember Ignatius. Ignorant among the doctors of Alcala; poor, penniless, among the students of Paris; persecuted, slandered...

That's the way: love, and have faith, and... suffer! Your love and your faith and your cross are the unfailing means to make effective and to perpetuate the ardent desires for apostolate that you bear in your heart.

475 You realize you are weak. And so, indeed, you are. In spite of all that— rather, because of it—God has sought you. He always uses inadequate instruments so that the work may be seen to be his.

From you he asks only docility.

476 When you *really* give yourself to God, no difficulty will be able to shake your optimism.

477 Why do you neglect those corners in your heart? As long as you don't give yourself completely, you can't expect to win others.

What a poor instrument you are!

478   But, surely—at this stage—you don't mean to tell me you need the approval, the favor, the encouragement of the powerful, to go on doing what God wants?

The powerful are often changeable, and you have to be constant. Be grateful if they help you, but go your way if they show you contempt.

479   Don't let it bother you. The "prudent" have always called the works of God madness.

Onward! Be daring!

480   Do you see? That cable—strand upon strand, many of them woven tightly together—is strong enough to lift enormous weights.

You and your brothers, with wills united to carry out God's will, can overcome all obstacles.

481   When you seek only God, and want to forward a work of zeal, you can very well practise that principle stated by a good friend of ours. "Spend all you ought, though you owe all you spend."

482   What does it matter if the whole world with all its power is against you? Forward!

Repeat the words of the psalm: "The Lord is my light and my salvation; whom shall I fear?....*Si consistant adversum me castra, non timebit cor meum*—If armies in camp should stand together against me, my heart shall not fear."

483   Courage! You can! Don't you see what God's grace did to that sleepy, cowardly Peter, who had denied him...to that fierce, relentless Paul, who had persecuted him?

484   Be an instrument of gold or of
steel, of platinum or of iron—big or small,
delicate or rough. They're all useful. Each
serves its own purpose. Who would dare
say that the carpenter's saw is any less
useful than the surgeon's scalpel?

Your duty is to be an instrument.

485   Well, so what? Unless your
motive is hidden pride (you think you're
perfect), I don't understand how you
can give up that work for souls just
because God's fire which first attracted
you, besides giving the light and warmth
that aroused your enthusiasm, should
also at times produce the smoke that
results from the weakness of the instrument!

486   Work. It's there. The instruments can't be left to grow rusty. There
are also "norms" to avoid the mildew and
the rust. Just put them into practice.

487   Don't worry about the financial difficulties in store for your apostolic undertaking. Have greater confidence in God; do all that your human means permit, and you'll see how soon money ceases to be a difficulty!

488   Don't let the lack of "instruments" stop your work. Begin as well as you can. As time passes, the function will create the organ. Some instruments formerly worthless, will become suitable. The rest can undergo a surgical operation, even though it be painful (there were no better "surgeons" than the saints!) and the work will go on.

489   A keen and living faith. A faith like Peter's. When you have it—our Lord has said so—you will move mountains, humanly insuperable obstacles that rise up against your apostolic undertakings.

490   An upright heart and good will.
With these, and your mind intent on carrying out what God wants, you will see
your dreams of Love come true and your
hunger for souls satisfied.

491   *"Nonne hic est fabri filius?
Nonne hic est faber, filius Mariae?"*—"Is
not this the carpenter's son? Is not this the
carpenter, the son of Mary?

This, said of Jesus, may very well be
said of you, with a bit of amazement and
a bit of mockery, when you *really* decide
to carry out the will of God, to be an
instrument: "But isn't this the one...?"

Say nothing, and let your works confirm your mission.

OUR LADY

492   The love of our Mother will be the breath that kindles into a living flame the embers of virtue that are hidden under the ashes of your indifference.

493   Love our Lady. And she will obtain abundant grace to help you conquer in your daily struggle. And the enemy will gain nothing by those perversities that seem to boil up continually within you, trying to engulf in their fragrant corruption the high ideals, those sublime commands that Christ himself has placed in your heart. *"Serviam!"*—"I will serve!"

494   Be Mary's, and you will be ours.

495   To Jesus we always go, and to him we always return, through Mary.

496   How men like to be reminded of their relationship with distinguished figures in literature, in politics, in the armed forces, in the Church!

Sing to Mary Immaculate, reminding her:

Hail Mary, daughter of God the Father! Hail Mary, Mother of God the Son! Hail Mary, Spouse of God the Holy Spirit! Greater than you—no one but God!

497   Say to her: Mother of mine—yours, because you are hers on many counts—may your love bind me to your Son's cross; may I not lack the faith, nor the courage, nor the daring, to carry out the will of our Jesus.

498   All the sins of your life seem to be rising up against you. Don't give up

hope! On the contrary, call your holy
mother Mary, with the faith and abandonment of a child. She will bring peace to
your soul.

499   Mary most holy, Mother of
God, passes unnoticed, just as one more
among the women of her town.

Learn from her how to live with "naturalness."

500   Wear on your breast the holy
scapular of Carmel. There are many excellent Marian devotions, but few are as
deep-rooted among the faithful and so
richly blessed by the popes. Besides, how
motherly is the sabbatine privilege!

501   When you were asked which
image of our Lady aroused your devotion
most, and you answered with the air of
long experience, "all of them", I realized
that you are a good son. That's why you

are equally moved—"they make me fall in love," you said—by *all* the pictures of your Mother.

502   Mary, teacher of prayer. See how she asks her Son at Cana. And how she insists, confidently, perseveringly... And how she succeeds.

Learn.

503   The loneliness of Mary. Alone! She weeps, forsakenly.

You and I should keep Our Lady company, and weep also: for Jesus has been fastened to the wood, with nails, our miseries.

504   The holy Virgin Mary, Mother of fair love, will bring relief to your heart, when it feels as if it's made of flesh, if you have recourse to her with confidence.

505   Love of our Lady is proof of a good spirit, in works and in individuals.

Don't trust the undertaking that lacks this characteristic.

506   Our Lady of sorrows. When you contemplate her, look into her heart: she is a Mother with two sons, face to face: him...and you.

507   What humility, that of my holy Mother Mary! She's not to be seen amidst the palms of Jerusalem, nor—except that first one at Cana—at the hour of the great miracles.

But she doesn't flee from the degradation of Golgotha: there she stands, *"juxta crucem Iesu"*—"by the cross of Jesus"—his Mother.

508   Marvel at the courage of Mary—at the foot of the cross, in the greatest of human sorrow (there is no sorrow like hers) filled with fortitude.

And ask her for that same fortitude, so that you, too, will know how to remain close to the cross.

509   Mary, teacher of the sacrifice that is hidden and silent.

See her, nearly always in the background, cooperating with her Son: she knows and remains silent.

510   See the simplicity? *"Ecce ancilla!"*—"Behold the handmaid!" And the Word was made flesh.

That's how the saints worked: without any outward show. And if there was any, it was in spite of themselves.

511   *"Ne timeas, Maria!"*—"Do not be afraid, Mary!"—Our Lady was troubled at the presence of the archangel!

And I want to throw away those safeguards of modesty that are the shield of my purity!

512 O Mother, Mother! With that word of yours, *"Fiat"*—"Be it done"—you have made us brothers of God and heirs to his glory. Blessed are you!

513 Before, by yourself, you couldn't. Now, you've turned to our Lady, and with her, how easy!

514 Have confidence. Return. Invoke our Lady and you'll be faithful.

515 So your strength is failing you? Why don't you tell your Mother about it: *"consolatrix afflictorum, auxilium christianorum..., Spes nostra, Regina apostolorum"*—"comforter of the afflicted, help of Christians..., our Hope, Queen of apostles!"

516 Mother! Call her with a loud voice. She is listening to you; she sees you in danger, perhaps, and she—your holy mother Mary—offers you, along with the grace of her son, the refuge of her arms, the tenderness of her embrace...and you will find yourself with added strength for the new battle.

THE CHURCH

517 *"Et unam, sanctam, catholicam et apostolicam Ecclesiam!"* I can well understand that pause of yours as you pray, savoring the words: "I believe in the Church, one, holy, catholic and apostolic."

518 What joy to be able to say with all the fervor of my soul: I love my Mother, the holy Church!

519 *"Serviam!"*—"I will serve!" That cry is your determination to serve the Church of God faithfully, even at the cost of fortune, of honor and of life.

520   Catholic, apostolic, Roman! I want you to be very Roman, ever anxious to make your "pilgrimage" to Rome "*videre Petrum*"—"to see Peter."

521   How good Christ was to leave the sacraments to his Church! They are a remedy for all our needs.

Venerate them and be very grateful, both to our Lord and to his Church.

522   Show veneration and respect for the holy liturgy of the Church and for its ceremonies. Observe them faithfully. Don't you see that, for us poor humans, even what is greatest and most noble enters through the senses?

523   The Church sings, it has been said, because just speaking would not satisfy its desires for prayer. You, as a Christian—and a chosen Christian—should learn to sing the liturgical chant.

524 "Let's burst into song!" said a soul in love, after seeing the wonders that our Lord was working through his ministry.

And the same advice I give to you: Sing! Let your grateful enthusiasm for your God overflow into joyous song.

525 To be "Catholic" means to love our country, and to let nobody surpass us in that love. And at the same time, it means to hold as our own the noble aspirations of all the other lands. How many glories of France are glories of mine! And in the same way, many things that make Germans proud—and Italians, British, Americans and Asians and Africans—are also sources of pride to me.

Catholic! A great heart, an open mind.

526 If you don't have the highest reverence for the priesthood and for the religious state, you certainly don't love God's Church.

527 That woman in the house of Simon the leper in Bethany, anointing the Master's head with precious ointment, reminds us of the duty to be generous in the worship of God.

All the richness, majesty and beauty possible would still seem too little to me.

And against those who attack the richness of sacred vessels, of vestments and altars, we hear the praise given by Jesus: *"opus enim bonum operata est in me"*— "She has done me a good turn."

HOLY MASS

528   A very important characteristic of the apostolic man is his love for the Mass.

529   "The Mass is long," you say, and I reply: "Because your love is short."

530   Many Christians take their time and have leisure enough in their social life (no hurry here). They are leisurely, too, in their professional activities, at table and recreation (no hurry here either). But isn't it strange how those same Christians find themselves in such a rush and want to hurry the priest, in their anxiety to shorten the time devoted to the most holy sacrifice of the altar?

531   "Treat him well for me, treat him well," said a certain elderly bishop with tears in his eyes to the priests he had just ordained.

Lord, I wish I had the voice and the authority to cry out in the same way to the ears and the hearts of many, many Christians!

532   How that saintly young priest, who was found worthy of martyrdom, wept at the foot of the altar as he thought of a soul who had come to receive Christ in the state of mortal sin!

Is that how you offer him reparation?

533   The humility of Jesus: in Bethlehem, in Nazareth, on Calvary. But still more humiliation and more self-abase-

ment in the most sacred host—more than
in the stable, more than in Nazareth, more
than on the cross.

That is why I must love the Mass so!
(*Our* Mass, Jesus.)

534 Receiving communion every
day for so many years! Anybody else
would be a saint by now—you told me—
and I...I'm always the same!

Son, I replied, keep up your daily
communion, and think: What would I be
if I hadn't received?

535 Communion, union, communication, intimacy: Word, bread, love.

536 Receive. It's not a lack of respect. Receive today precisely when you
have just got over that "bit of trouble".

Have you forgotten what Jesus said? It
is not those who are well but those who
are sick who need the physician.

537   When you approach the tabernacle remember that *he* has been waiting for you for twenty centuries.

538   There he is: King of Kings and Lord of Lords, hidden in the bread.

To this extreme has he humbled himself for love of you.

539   He's here on earth for *you*. Don't think it's reverence to stay away from communion, if you are prepared to receive. The only irreverence is to receive him unworthily.

540   What a source of grace there is in spiritual communion! Practise it frequently and you'll have greater presence of God and closer union with him in all your actions.

541   Piety has its own good manners. Learn them. It's a shame to see those

"pious" people who don't know how to
assist at Mass—even those who hear it
daily—nor how to bless themselves (they
make some weird gestures very hurriedly),
nor how to bend their knee before the
tabernacle (their ridiculous genuflections
seem a mockery), nor how to bow their
heads reverently before an image of our
Lady.

542   Don't put up those mass-pro-
duced statues for public devotion. I prefer
a rough, wrought-iron figure of Christ to
those colored, plaster statues that look as
if they were made of sugar candy.

543   You saw me celebrate holy
Mass on a plain altar without any decora-
tion behind it. The crucifix was large, the
candlesticks heavy, with thick candles of
graded height, sloping up toward the
cross.

The frontal, the liturgical color of the
day; a sweeping chasuble; the chalice,

rich, simple in its lines, with a broad cup.
We had no electric light, nor did we miss
it.

And you found it difficult to leave the
oratory. You felt at home there. Do you
see how we are led to God, brought close
to him, by the liturgy of the Catholic
Church?

COMMUNION
OF THE SAINTS

544 The communion of the saints. How shall I explain it to you? You know what blood transfusions can do for the body? Well, that's what the communion of the saints does for the soul.

545 Live a special communion of the saints, and at the moment of interior struggle, as well as during the long hours of your work, each of you will feel the joy and the strength of not being alone.

546 Son, how well you live the communion of the saints when you wrote:

"Yesterday I 'felt' that you were praying for me!"

547   Someone else who knows of this "communication" of supernatural riches told me: "That letter did me a world of good: I could feel everyone's prayers behind it...and I very much need to be prayed for."

548   If you feel the communion of the saints—if you live it—you'll gladly be a man of penance. And you will realize that penance is "*gaudium, etsi laboriosum*"—"joy in spite of hardship," and you will feel yourself "allied" to all the penitent souls that have been, that are, and that ever will be.

549   You will find it easier to do your duty if you think of how many brothers are helping you, and of the help you fail to give them when you are not faithful.

550   "*Ideo omnia sustineo propter electos*"—"I bear all things for the sake of the elect," "*ut et ipsi salutem consequantur*"—"that they also may obtain the salvation," "*quae est in Christo Iesu*"—"that is in Christ Jesus."

What a good way to live the communion of the saints! Ask our Lord to give you that spirit of St Paul.

DEVOTIONS

551   Flee from routine as from the devil himself. The great means to avoid falling into that abyss, the grave of true piety, is the constant presence of God.

552   Have only a few private devotions, but be constant in them.

553   Don't forget your childhood prayers, learned perhaps from your mother's lips. Say them each day with simplicity, as you did then.

554   Don't omit your visits to the blessed sacrament. After saying your usual prayer tell Jesus, really present in the tabernacle, about the cares and worries of your day. And he will give you light and courage for your life as a Christian.

555   How truly lovable is the sacred humanity of our God! Having placed yourself in the most holy wound of your Lord's right hand, you asked me: "If one of Christ's wounds cleans, heals, soothes, strengthens, kindles, and enraptures, what wouldn't the five do as they lie open on the cross?"

556   The way of the cross. Here indeed is a strong and fruitful devotion! May you make it a habit to go over those fourteen points of our Lord's passion and death each Friday. I assure you that you'll gain strength for the whole week.

557   Christmas devotions. I don't frown when I see you making the imitation mountains of the crib, and placing the simple clay figures around the manger. You have never seemed more a man to me than now, when you are so like a child.

558   The holy Rosary is a powerful weapon. Use it with confidence and you'll be amazed at the results.

559   St Joseph, a father to Christ, is also your father and your lord. Have recourse to him.

560   St Joseph, our father and lord, is a teacher of the interior life. Put yourself under his patronage and you'll feel the effect of his power.

561   Speaking of St Joseph in her autobiography, St Teresa writes: "Whoever fails to find a master to teach him how to pray should choose this glorious saint for a master; and he will not go astray."

This advice comes from an experienced soul. Follow it.

562　　Have confidence in your guardian angel. Treat him as a very dear friend—that's what he is—and he will do a thousand services for you in the ordinary affairs of each day.

563　　Win over the guardian angel of the one you want to draw to your apostolate. He is always a great "accomplice".

564　　If you would remember the presence of your guardian angel and those of your neighbors, you would avoid many of the foolish things you let slip into your conversation.

565　　You seem amazed because your guardian angel has done so many obvious favors for you. But you shouldn't be: that's why our Lord has placed him at your side.

566   You say there are many occasions of going astray in such surroundings? That's true, but aren't there any guardian angels as well?

567   Turn to your guardian angel at the moment of trial; he will protect you from the devil and bring you holy inspirations.

568   How joyfully the holy guardian angels must have obeyed that soul who said to them: "Holy angels, I call upon you, like the spouse of the Canticle of Canticles, '*ut nuntietis ei quia amore langueo*'—'to tell him that I am dying with love.' "

569   I know you will be glad to have this prayer to the holy guardian angels of our tabernacles:

O angelic spirits, who guard our tabernacles, wherein lies the adorable treasure of the holy eucharist, defend it from profanation and preserve it for our love.

570 Drink at the clear fountain of the *Acts of the Apostles*. In the twelfth chapter, Peter is freed from prison by the ministry of angels and comes to the house of Mark's mother. Those inside don't want to believe the servant girl when she tells them Peter is at the door. "*Angelus eius est!*"—"It's his angel!" they say.

See on what intimate terms the early Christians were with their guardian angels.

And what about you?

571 The holy souls in purgatory. Out of charity, out of justice, and out of an excusable selfishness (they have such power with God!) remember them often in your sacrifices and in your prayers.

Whenever you speak of them, may you be able to say, "My good friends, the souls in purgatory."

572   You ask me why I always recommend so insistently the daily use of holy water. I could give you many reasons. This one of the saint of Avila would surely suffice for you: "From nothing do evil spirits flee more, never to return, than from holy water."

573   Thank you, my God, for placing in my heart such love for the pope.

574   Who told you it's not manly to make novenas? These devotions can be very manly if it is a man who does them, in a spirit of prayer and penance.

573. You ask me why I always recommend... occ... the... obscure to
help when I could give you many reasons. Throuts of the saint of A..., would
surely suffice for you. From nothing do
I... think figures ... to retain ... than
from holy water ...

574. I thank you to God for placing
in my heart such love for the pope.

575. Who told you it is not enough to
make a novena? These devotions can be
very ... to many [for] a man who does them ...
in a spirit of prayer and penance ...

FAITH

575 There are some who pass through life as through a tunnel: they fail to realize the splendor and the security and the warmth of the sun of faith.

576 With what infamous lucidity does Satan argue against our Catholic faith!

But, let's tell him always, without entering into debate: I am a child of the Church.

577 You feel yourself with gigantic faith. He who gives you that faith will give you the means.

578   It is St Paul who tells you, apostolic soul: *"Iustus ex fide vivit"*—"He who is just lives by faith."

How is it that you're letting that fire die down?

579   Faith. It's a pity to see how frequently many Christians have it on their lips and yet how sparingly they put it into their actions.

You would think it a virtue to be preached only, and not one to be practised.

580   Humbly ask God to increase your faith. Then, with new lights, you'll see clearly the difference between the world's paths and your way as an apostle.

581   How humbly and simply the evangelists relate incidents that show up the weak and wavering faith of the apostles!

This is to keep you and me from giving up the hope of some day achieving the strong and unshakeable faith that those same apostles had later.

582   How beautiful is our Catholic faith! It provides a solution for all our anxieties; it gives peace to the mind and fills the heart with hope.

583   I'm not miracle-minded. As I've told you, I can find more than enough miracles in the holy Gospel to confirm my faith.

But I can't help pitying those Christians, many of them pious people, "apostles" even, who smile when people speak of extraordinary ways, supernatural events. I feel the urge to tell them: Yes, this is still the age of miracles. We, too, would work them if we had enough faith!

584   Stir up the fire of your faith! Christ is not a figure of the past. He is not a memory lost in history.

He lives! *"Iesus Christus heri et hodie: ipse et in saecula!"* As St Paul says "Jesus Christ is the same yesterday and today—yes, and forever!"

585   *"Si habueritis fidem, sicut granum sinapis!"*—"If you have faith like a grain of mustard seed...!"

What promises are contained in this exclamation of the Master!

586   God is always the same. It is men of faith that are needed: then there will be a renewal of the wonders we read of in the holy Scriptures.

"Ecce non est abbreviata manus Domini"—"The hand of God the Lord"—his power—"has not grown weaker!"

587   They have no faith, but they do have superstitions. We laughed, and at the same time we're sorry, when that tough character became alarmed at the sight of a black cat or at hearing a certain word which of itself meant nothing but for him was a bad omen.

588   *"Omnia possibilia sunt credenti"*—"All things are possible for him who believes." The words are Christ's. How is it that you don't say to him with the apostles: *"Adauge nobis fidem!"*—"Increase my faith!"

HUMILITY

589 When you hear the plaudits of triumph, let there also sound in your ears the laughter you provoked with your failures.

590 Don't aspire to be like the gilded weather vane on top of a great building. However much it may glitter, however high it may be, it adds nothing to the firmness of the structure.

Rather be like an old stone block hidden in the foundations, under the ground where no one can see you. Because of you, the house will not fall.

591 The more I am exalted, my Jesus the more you must humble me in my heart, showing me what I've been and what I'll be if you forsake me.

592   Don't forget that you are just a trash can. So if by any chance the divine gardener should lay his hands on you, and scrub and clean you, and fill you with magnificent flowers, neither the scent nor the colors that beautify your ugliness should make you proud.

Humble yourself: don't you know that you are a trash can?

593   The day you see yourself as you are, you will think it natural to be despised by others.

594   You're not humble when you humble yourself, but when you are humbled by others and you bear it for Christ.

595   If you really knew yourself, you would rejoice at being despised, and your heart would weep in the face of honors and praise.

596   Don't feel hurt when others see your faults. What should really distress you is the offense against God and the scandal you may give.

Apart from that, may you be known for what you are and be despised. Don't be sorry if you are nothing, because then Jesus will have to put everything into you.

597   If you were to obey the impulse of your heart and the dictates of reason, you would always lie flat on the ground, prostrate, a vile worm, ugly and miserable in the sight of that God who puts up with so much from you!

598   How great is the value of humility! *"Quia respexit humilitatem..."*—"Because he has regarded the lowliness..." It is not of her faith, nor of her charity, nor of her immaculate purity that our Mother speaks in the house of Zachary. Her joyful hymn sings:

"Because he has regarded the lowliness of his handmaid, behold: henceforth all generations shall call me blessed."

599   You are dust, fallen and dirty. Even though the breath of the Holy Spirit should lift you above all earthly things and make you shine like gold—your misery reflecting in those heights the sovereign rays of the Sun of Justice—don't forget the lowliness of your state.

An instant of pride would cast you back to the ground; and having been light, you would again become dirt.

600   You,...proud? About what?

601   Pride? Why? Before long (maybe years, maybe days) you'll be a heap of rotting flesh, worms, foul-smelling fluids, your shroud in filthy shreds...and no one on earth will remember you.

602   For all your learning, all your fame, all your eloquence and power, if you're not humble, you're worth nothing. Cut out that ego that dominates you so completely—root it out. God will help you. And then you'll be able to begin to work for Christ in the lowest place in his army of apostles.

603   That false humility is laziness. Such a "humbleness" leads you to give up rights that really are duties.

604   Humbly acknowledge your weakness. Then you can say with the Apostle: *"Cum enim infirmor, tunc potens sum"*—"For when I am weak, then I am strong."

605   "Father, how can you stand such filth?" you asked me after a contrite confession.

I said nothing, thinking that if your humility makes you feel like that—like filth, a heap of filth!—then we may yet turn all your weakness into something really great.

606   See how humble our Jesus is: a donkey was his throne in Jerusalem!

607   Humility is one of the good ways to achieve interior peace. He has said so: "Learn of me, for I am meek and humble of heart, and you will find rest for your souls."

608   It's not lack of humility to be aware of your soul's progress. That way you can thank God for it.

But don't forget that you are a beggar, wearing a good suit...on loan.

609   Self-knowledge leads us by the hand, as it were, to humility.

610   Your firm defense of the spirit and norms of the apostolate in which you work should never falter through false humility. That firmness is not pride: it's the cardinal virtue of fortitude.

611   It was because of pride. You thought you were already capable of everything—all by yourself. But then he left you for a moment and you fell—headlong.

Be humble, and his extraordinary aid will not fail you.

612   Get rid of those proud thoughts! You are but the brush in the hand of the artist, and nothing more.

Tell me, what is a brush good for if it doesn't let the artist do his work?

613   So that you'll be humble—you, who are so self-satisfied and empty—it's enough to consider these words of Isaias: You're a drop of water or dew that falls on the earth and is scarcely seen.

OBEDIENCE

614 In apostolic work there is no such thing as a trifling disobedience.

615 Temper your will. Strengthen your will. With God's grace, let it be like a sword of steel.

Only by being strong-willed can you know how not to be so in order to obey.

616 With that slowness, with that passivity, with that reluctance to obey, what damage you do to the apostolate and what satisfaction you give the enemy!

617 Obey, as an instrument obeys in the hands of the artist—not stopping to consider the why and the wherefore of what it is doing. Be sure that you'll never be directed to do anything that isn't good and for the greater glory of God.

618 The enemy: "Will you obey, even in this ridiculous little detail?"

You with God's grace: "I will obey, even in this *heroic* little detail!"

619 Initiative. You must have it in your apostolate, within the limits of your instructions.

If your projects exceed those limits or if you're in doubt, consult your superior, without telling anyone else your thoughts.

Never forget: You are only an agent.

620 If obedience doesn't give you peace, it's because you're proud.

621 What a pity if the one in charge doesn't give you good example! But is it only for his personal qualities that you obey? Or do you in your selfishness interpret St Paul's *"obedite praepositis vestris"*—"Obey your superiors" with an addition of your own: "Always provided they have virtues to my own taste?"

622 How well you understand obedience when you write: "Always to obey is to be a martyr without dying!"

623 You've been told to do something that seems difficult and useless. Do it. And you'll see that it's easy and fruitful.

624 Hierarchy: Each piece in its place. What would be left of a Velazquez painting if each color were to go out of its place, each thread of the canvas were to break apart, each piece of the wooden frame were to separate itself from the others?

625   Your obedience is not worthy of the name unless you are ready to abandon your most flourishing work whenever someone with authority so commands.

626   Isn't it true, Lord, that you were greatly consoled by the child-like remark of that man who, disconcerted by having to obey in something unpleasant and repulsive, whispered to you: "Jesus, may I put on a good face!"

627   Yours should be a silent obedience. That tongue!

628   Right now, when you are finding it hard to obey, remember your Lord, *"factus obediens usque ad mortem, mortem autem crucis"*—"obedient unto death, even to death on the cross!"

629   Oh, the power of obedience! The lake of Genesareth had denied its fishes to Peter's nets. A whole night in vain.

Then, obedient, he lowered his net again into the water and they caught *"piscium multitudinem copiosam"*—"a great number of fishes."

Believe me, the miracle is repeated every day.

POVERTY

630 Don't forget it: he has most who needs least. Don't create needs for yourself.

631 Detach yourself from the goods of this world. Love and practice poverty of spirit: be content with what is sufficient for leading a simple and temperate life.

Otherwise, you'll never be an apostle.

632 True poverty is not to lack things but to be detached, to give up voluntarily one's dominion over them.

That's why some poor people are really rich...and vice versa.

633   As a man of God, put the same effort into scorning riches that men of the world put into possessing them.

634   What an attachment to the things of the world! But soon they will slip from your grasp, for the rich man cannot carry his riches with him to the grave.

635   You don't have the spirit of poverty if you don't select for yourself what is worst, when you are able to choose in such a way that it will not be noticed.

636   *"Divitiae, si affluant, nolite cor apponere"*—"If riches abound, set not your heart upon them." Strive, rather, to use them generously—and, if necessary, heroically.

Be poor of spirit.

637   You don't love poverty if you don't love what poverty brings with it.

638   What holy resources poverty has!

Do you remember? It was a time of financial stress in your apostolic undertaking. You had given without stint down to the last penny. Then that priest of God said to you: "I, too, will give you all I have." You knelt and you heard, "May the blessing of almighty God, the Father, the Son and the Holy Spirit, descend upon you and remain with you forever!"

You are still convinced that you were well paid.

DISCRETION

639   Remain silent, and you will never regret it. Speak, and you often will.

640   How can you dare ask others to keep your secret, when that very request is a sign that you aren't able to keep it yourself?

641   Discretion is neither mystery nor secrecy. It is simply naturalness.

642   Discretion is..."fineness of spirit". Don't you feel annoyed and uncomfortable deep down inside when the affairs of your family, honorable and ordinary, emerge from the warmth of the home into the indifference or curiosity of the public gaze?

643   Be slow to reveal the intimate details of your apostolate. Don't you see that the world in its selfishness will fail to understand?

644   Be silent! Don't forget that your ideal is like a newly-lit flame. A single breath might be enough to put it out in your heart.

645   How fruitful is silence! All the energy you lose through your failures in discretion is energy taken from the effectiveness of your work.

Be discreet.

646   If you were more discreet, you would not have to complain within yourself about the bad taste left by so many of your conversations.

647 Don't seek to be "understood". That lack of understanding is providential: so that your sacrifice may pass unnoticed.

648 If you hold your tongue, you'll gain greater effectiveness in your apostolic undertakings (so many people let their strength slip through their mouths!) and you'll avoid many dangers of vainglory.

649 Always display! You ask me for pictures, charts and statistics.

I won't send you what you ask, because (though I respect the opposite opinion) I would then think I had acted with a view to making good on earth, and where I want to make good is in heaven.

650 There are many people, holy people, who don't understand your way. Don't strive to make them understand. It would be a waste of time and would give rise to indiscretions.

651   "What gives life to roots and branches is the sap, which always works on the inside."

Your friend who wrote those words knew you were nobly ambitious. And he showed you the way: discretion and sacrifice—"working on the inside!"

652   Discretion, a virtue of the few.

Who slandered women by saying that discretion is not a woman's virtue? How many men—yes, red-blooded men—have yet to learn!

653   What an example of discretion the Mother of God has given us! Not even to St Joseph does she communicate the mystery.

Ask our Lady for the discretion you lack.

654   Bitterness has sharpened your tongue. Be silent!

655   I cannot overemphasize the importance of discretion.

If it isn't the blade of your sword, at least it's the hilt.

656   Always remain silent when you feel indignation surge up within you—even when you have reason to be angry.

For in spite of your discretion, you always say more than you want to in such moments.

JOY

657   True virtue is not sad and repulsive, but pleasantly joyful.

658   If things go well let's rejoice, blessing God, who makes them prosper. And if they go wrong? Let's rejoice, blessing God, who allows us to share the sweetness of his cross.

659   The cheerfulness you should have is not the kind we might call physiological—like that of a healthy animal. Rather, it is the supernatural happiness that comes from the abandonment of everything, including yourself, into the loving arms of our Father God.

660   If you're an apostle you should never feel discouraged. There is no obstacle that you cannot overcome.

Then why are you sad?

661   Long faces, coarse manners, a ridiculous appearance, a repelling air. Is that how you hope to inspire others to follow Christ?

662   You are unhappy? Think: there must be an obstacle between God and me. You will seldom be wrong.

663   You ask me to suggest a cure for your sadness. I'll give you a prescription from an expert adviser, the apostle St James:

"Tristatus aliquis vestrum?"—"Are you sad, my son?" *"Oret!"*—"Pray!" Try it and you will see.

664   Don't be sad. Let your outlook be more..."ours"—more christian.

665 I want you always to be happy, for cheerfulness is an essential part of your way.

Pray that the same supernatural joy may be granted to us all.

666 "*Laetetur cor quaerentium Dominum*"—"Let the hearts of them rejoice who seek the Lord."

There you have light to help you discover the reasons for your sadness.

OTHER VIRTUES

667 Acts of faith, hope and love are valves which provide an outlet for the fire of those souls who live the life of God.

668 Do everything unselfishly, for pure love, as if there were neither reward nor punishment. But in your heart foster the glorious hope of heaven.

669 It's good that you serve God as a son, without payment—generously. But don't worry if at times you think of the reward.

670 Jesus says: "Everyone who has left house or brothers or sisters or father

or mother or wife or children or lands, for
my name's sake, shall receive a hundredfold and shall possess life everlasting."

Try to find anyone on earth who repays
with such generosity!

671   "Jesus remains silent."—"*Iesus
autem tacebat*." Why do you speak, to
console yourself or to explain yourself?

Say nothing. Seek joy in contempt:
you'll always receive less than you deserve. Can you, by any chance, ask: "*Quid
enim mali feci?*"—"What evil have I
done?"

672   You can be sure you're a man
of God if you suffer injustice gladly and
in silence.

673   What a beautiful answer was
given by a certain venerable man to his
young friend who complained of an injus-

tice he had suffered: "Does it hurt you?" he asked. "Then, don't desire to be good!"

674 Never give your opinion if you're not asked for it, even though you may think it is the best one.

675 It's true that he was a sinner. But don't pass so final a judgment. Have pity in your heart and don't forget that he may yet be an Augustine, while you remain just another mediocrity.

676 All the things of this world are no more than dirt. Place them in a heap under your feet and you'll be so much nearer to heaven.

677 Gold, silver, jewels: dirt, piles of manure.

Delights, sensual pleasures, satisfactions of the appetites: like a beast, like a mule, like a hog, like a cock, like a bull...

Honors, distinctions, titles: things of air, puffs of pride, lies, nothingness.

678 Don't set your heart on things here below. Such love is selfish. A few short hours after God calls you into his presence, those you love will recoil from you in horror and revulsion.

Elsewhere is the love that endures.

679 Gluttony is an ugly vice. Don't you feel a bit amused and even a bit disgusted when you see a group of distinguished gentlemen seated solemnly around a table, stuffing fatty foods into their digestive tubes with an air of ritual, as if the whole thing were an end in itself?

680 Don't talk about food at the table. That's a lack of refinement unworthy of you. Speak about noble things—of the mind, of the soul—and you'll have dignified this duty.

681   The day you leave the table without having made some small mortification, you will have eaten like a pagan.

682   Ordinarily you eat more than you need. And the natural result, a heavy fullness and discomfort, benumbs your mind and renders you unfit to savor supernatural treasures.

What a fine virtue temperance is, even by earthly standards!

683   I see you, christian gentleman (that's what you say you are), kissing an image, muttering some vocal prayer, crying out against those who attack the Church of God, even frequenting the holy sacraments.

But I don't see you making a sacrifice, nor avoiding certain conversations of a worldly nature (I could with justice have used another adjective!), nor being generous toward those in need (including that

same Church of God!), nor putting up with
a failing in one of your brothers, nor
checking your pride for the sake of the
common good, nor getting rid of that tight
cloak of selfishness, nor...so many other
things!

Yes, I see you...But I don't see you...
And yet, you say you are a christian
gentleman! What a poor idea you have of
Christ!

684   So your talents, your personality, your qualities are being wasted. So
you're not allowed to take full advantage
of them.

Meditate well on these words of a spiritual writer: "The incense offered to God is
not wasted. Our Lord is more honored by
the immolation of your talents than by
their vain use."

TRIBULATIONS

685 The storm of persecution is good. What is lost? You can't lose something if it's already lost.

When the whole tree is not torn up by the roots—and there is no wind or hurricane that can uproot the tree of the Church—only the dry branches fall. And it is best that they fall.

686 All right: that person has behaved badly toward you. But, haven't you behaved worse toward God?

687 Jesus: wherever you have passed not a heart has remained indifferent. You are either loved or hated.

When an apostolic man follows you, carrying out his duty, is it surprising—if he is another Christ!—that he should provoke similar murmurs of aversion or of love?

688   Once again, they've been talking, they've written—in favor, against; with good, and with not so good will; insinuations and slanders, panegyrics and plaudits; hits and misses...

Fool, big fool! As long as you keep going straight toward your target—head and heart intoxicated with God—why care about the clamor of the wind or the chirping of the cricket, or the bellowing, or the grunting, or the neighing?

Besides, it's inevitable; don't try to install doors in open air.

689   Tongues have been wagging and you've suffered rebuffs that hurt you, and all the more because you were not expecting them.

Your supernatural reaction should be to pardon—and even to *ask* for pardon!— and to take advantage of the experience to detach yourself from creatures.

690 When you meet with suffering, contempt, ...the cross, your thoughts should be: what is this compared to what I deserve?

691 Are you suffering some great tribulation? Do you have reverses? Say very slowly, as if savoring the words, this powerful and manly prayer:

"May the most just and most lovable will of God be done, be fulfilled, be praised and eternally exalted above all things. Amen. Amen."

I assure you that you'll find peace.

692 You suffer in this present life, which is only a dream, and a short one at that. Rejoice, because your Father God loves you so much, and if you put no

obstacles in his way, after this bad dream
he will give you a good awakening.

693   It hurt you not to have been
thanked for that favor. Answer me these
two questions: Are you so grateful toward
Christ Jesus? Did you really do that favor
in the hope of being thanked for it on
earth?

694   I don't know why you're
amazed: the enemies of Christ were never
very reasonable.

When Lazarus was raised from the
dead, you might have thought they would
yield and confess the divinity of Jesus. But
no! "Let us kill him who gives life!" they
said.

It's the same today.

695   In the moments of struggle and
tribulation, when perhaps the "good" fill
your way with obstacles, lift up your
apostolic heart: listen to Jesus as he speaks

of the grain of mustard seed and of the leaven, and say to him: "*Edissere nobis parabolam*"—"Explain the parable to me."

And you'll feel the joy of contemplating the victory to come: the birds of the air under the shelter of your apostolate, now only in its beginnings, and the whole of the meal leavened.

696 If you accept tribulation with a faint heart, you lose your joy and your peace, and you run the risk of not deriving any spiritual profit from that trial.

697 Public events have led you to prefer a voluntary confinement, which is worse perhaps, because of the circumstances, than the confinement of a prison. You've suffered an eclipse of your personality.

On all sides you feel yourself hemmed in: selfishness, curiosity, misunderstanding, gossip. Well, so what? Have you forgotten your very free will and that power of yours as a "child"? The absence of leaves and flowers (of external action) does not exclude the growth and activity of the roots (interior life).

Work: things will change and you'll yield more fruit than before—and it will be more savory.

698   So you've been hauled over the coals? Don't follow the advice of pride and lose your temper. Think: how charitable they are toward me! The things they've left unsaid!

699   Cross, toil, tribulation: such will be your lot as long as you live. That was the way Christ followed, and the disciple is not above his Master.

700   Agreed: there is a lot of external pressure, which excuses you in part. But there is also complicity within (take a good look), and there I see no excuse.

701   Have you not heard the parable of the vine and the branches from the lips of the Master? Console yourself: He demands much of you, for you are the branch that bears fruit. And he must prune you, "*ut fructum plus afferas*"—"so that you'll yield more fruit."

Of course that cutting—that pruning— hurts. But, afterwards, how luxuriant the growth, how fruitful your works!

702   You are upset. Look: happen what may in your interior life or in the world around you, never forget that the importance of events or of people is very relative. Take things calmly. Let time pass. And then, as you view persons and events dispassionately and from afar, you'll acquire the perspective that will enable you to see each thing in its proper place and in its true proportion.

If you do this, you'll be more objective and you'll be spared many a cause of anxiety.

703   A bad night in a bad inn. That's how St Teresa of Jesus is said to have described this earthly life. It's a good comparison, isn't it?

704   A visit to a famous monastery. A certain foreign lady was deeply moved on seeing the poverty of the place: "You lead a very hard life, don't you?" And the pleased monk merely replied, as if speaking to himself, "Just what you asked for, isn't it so? Now that you have it, don't let it go."

These words, which I joyfully heard that holy man say, I can only repeat to you with sorrow when you tell me you're not happy.

705   Worry? Never! That's to lose your peace.

706 Physical collapse. You are worn out...Stop that exterior activity. Rest. Consult a doctor. Obey, and don't worry.

You'll soon return to your normal life and, if you're faithful, you'll improve your apostolate.

INTERIOR STRUGGLE

707 Don't be troubled if, as you consider the marvels of the supernatural world, you hear that other voice—the intimate, insinuating voice of the "old man".

It's "the body of death" that cries out for its lost privileges. God's grace is sufficient for you: be faithful and you will conquer.

708 The world, the devil and the flesh are a band of adventurers who take advantage of the weakness of that savage you have within you. In exchange for the poor bauble of pleasure, which is worth nothing, they want you to hand over to them the pure gold and the pearls, the diamonds and the rubies, drenched in the living and redeeming blood of your God —the price and the treasure of your eternity.

709 Do you hear these words? "In another state in life, in another place, in another position or occupation, you would do much more good. Talent isn't needed for what you are doing."

Well, listen to me: Wherever you have been placed, you please God, ...and what you've just been thinking is clearly a suggestion of the devil.

710 You are worried and sad because your communions are cold and barren. Tell me, when you approach the sacrament, do you seek yourself or do you seek Jesus? If you seek yourself, there is reason indeed to be sad. But if you seek Christ—as you ought—could you want a surer sign than the cross to know you've found him?

711 Another fall...and what a fall! Despair? No! Humble yourself and through Mary, your Mother, have recourse to the merciful love of Jesus. A *miserere*—"have mercy on me"—and lift up your heart! And now, begin again.

712 How low you have fallen this time! Begin the foundations from down there. Be humble. *"Cor contritum et humiliatum, Deus, non despicies."*—"A contrite and humbled heart, O God, you will not despise."

713 You haven't set yourself against God. Your falls are due to weakness. All right, but those weaknesses are so frequent! You don't know how to avoid them, so that, even if you don't want me to consider you bad, I'll have to consider you both bad and stupid.

714   Yours is a desire without desire, as long as you don't put firmly aside the occasion of falling. Don't fool yourself telling me you're weak. You're a coward, which is not the same thing.

715   That confusion in your spirit, the temptation that envelops you, is like a blindfold over the eyes of your soul.

You are in the dark. Don't insist on walking by yourself, for by yourself you will fall. Go to your Director—to your superior—and he will make you hear once again those words of Raphael the Archangel to Tobias:

"Forti animo esto, in proximo est ut a Deo cureris."

"Take comfort; before long God will heal you." Be obedient and the scales, the blindfold, will fall from your eyes and God will fill you with grace and peace.

716   "I don't know how to conquer myself!" you write me despondently. And

I answer: But have you really tried to use the means?

717   Blessed be the hardships of this earth! Poverty, tears, hatred, injustice, dishonor...You can endure all things in him who strengthens you.

718   You suffer and you want to bear it in silence. It doesn't matter if you complain—it's the natural reaction of our poor flesh—as long as your will wants, now and always, only what God wants.

719   Never despair. Lazarus was dead and decaying: "*iam foetet, quatriduanus est enim*"—"by now he will smell; this is the fourth day," Martha told Jesus.

If you hear the inspiration of God and follow it—"*Lazare, veni foras!*"—"Lazarus, come forth!—you will return to Life.

720   It's hard! Yes, I know. But, forward! No one receives the reward—and what a reward!—except those who fight bravely.

721   If your spiritual edifice is tottering, or if everything seems to be up in the air, ...lean on filial confidence in Jesus and Mary; it's the firm and steady rock on which you should have built from the beginning.

722   This time the trial has been long. Perhaps—and without the perhaps—you haven't borne it well so far, for you were still seeking human consolations. But your Father God has torn them out by the roots so as to leave you no other refuge but him.

723   So you couldn't care less? Don't try to fool yourself. This very moment, if I were to ask you about persons and activities, in which for God's love you put your soul, I know that you would answer me eagerly, with the interest of one speaking of what is his own.

It's not true that you don't care. It's just that you're not tireless, and that you need more time for yourself: time that will also be for your work, since, after all, you are the instrument.

724 You tell me that in your heart you have fire and water, cold and heat, empty passions and God: one candle lit to St Michael and another to the devil.

Calm yourself. As long as you are willing to fight there are not two candles burning in your heart. There is only one: the archangel's.

725 The enemy nearly always works like that on the souls who are going to resist him: hypocritically, quietly, using spiritual motives, trying not to attract attention. And then, when there seems to be no way out (though there is), he comes brazenly, trying to bring on a despair like that of Judas—despair without repentance.

726   After losing those human consolations you have been left with a feeling of loneliness, as if you were hanging by a thin thread over the emptiness of a black abyss. And your cries, your shouts for help, seem to go unheard by anybody.

The truth is you deserve to be so forlorn. Be humble; don't seek yourself; don't seek your own satisfaction. Love the cross—to bear it is little—and our Lord will hear your prayer. And in time, calm will be restored to your senses. And your heart will heal, and you will have peace.

727   Your flesh is tender and raw. That's how you are. Everything seems to make you suffer in your mind and in your senses. And everything is a temptation to you...

Be humble—I insist. You will see how quickly all this passes. The pain will turn into joy, and the temptation into firm purpose.

But meanwhile, strengthen your faith; fill yourself with hope; and make constant acts of love, even though you think they come only from your lips.

728 All our fortitude is on loan.

729 Each day, O my God, I am less sure of myself and more sure of you!

730 If you don't leave him, he won't leave you.

731 Depend on Jesus for everything. You have nothing, are worth nothing, are capable of nothing. He will act, if you abandon yourself to him.

732   O Jesus! I rest in you.

733   Trust always in your God. He does not lose battles.

LAST THINGS

734 "This is your hour and the power of darkness." So, the sinner has his hour then? Yes...and God his eternity!

735 If you're an apostle, death will be a good friend who helps you on your way.

736 Have you seen the dead leaves fall in the sad autumn twilight? So fall souls each day into eternity. One day, the falling leaf will be you.

737 Haven't you heard the mournful tone with which the worldly complain that "each day that passes is a step nearer death"?

It is. And I tell you: rejoice, apostolic soul, for each day that passes brings you closer to Life.

738   For others, death is a stumbling block, a source of terror. For us, death—Life—is an encouragement and a stimulus.

For them it is the end; for us, the beginning.

739   Don't be afraid of death. Accept it from this day on, generously...when God wills it, how God wills it, where God wills it. Believe me, it will come at the time, in the place and in the way that are best—sent by your Father God. May our sister death be welcome!

740   What part of the world would collapse if I were missing, if I were to die?

741 Do you see how the corpse of a loved one disintegrates in foul and reeking fluids? Well, that is the body beautiful! Contemplate it and draw your own conclusions.

742 Those paintings by Valdez Leal,* with so much distinguished heap of decaying flesh—bishops, noblemen, all in rank corruption—surely they must move you.

What then do you say of the Duke of Gandia's** cry: "No more will I serve a lord whom I can lose through death!"?

743 You talk of dying "heroically". Don't you think that it is more heroic to die unnoticed, in a good bed, like a bourgeois, ...but to die of Love?

---

*Valdéz Leal: A Spanish painter famous for his pictures of the dead.

**Duke of Gandia: Later St Francis Borgia.

744   You—if you are an apostle—will not have to die. You will move to a new house, that's all.

745   "He shall come to judge the living and the dead." Thus we say in the Creed. May you never lose sight of that judgment and of that justice and...of that judge.

746   Doesn't your soul burn with the desire to make your Father God happy when he has to judge you?

747   There is a great tendency among worldly souls to think of God's mercy, and so they are emboldened to persist in their follies.

It's true that God our Lord is infinitely merciful, but he is also infinitely just; and there is a judgment, and he is the judge.

748   Courage. Don't you know that St Paul tells the Corinthians that "each one will receive his own wages according to his works"?

749   There is a hell. A trite enough statement, you think. I will repeat it, then: there is a hell!

Echo it, at the right moment, in the ears of one friend, and another, and another.

750   Listen to me, you who are up to your neck in science: your science cannot deny the reality of diabolic activities. My Mother, the holy Church, for many years—and it is also a praiseworthy private devotion—required the priests each day at the foot of the altar to invoke St Michael, *"contra nequitiam et insidias diaboli"*—"against the wickedness and snares of the devil."

751   Heaven: "The eye has not seen, nor the ear heard, neither has it entered into the heart of man what things God has prepared for them who love him."

Don't these revelations of the Apostle spur you on to fight?

752   Always. Forever! Words brought to our lips by the human desire to prolong—to make eternal—what is pleasant.

Lying words, on earth, where everything must end.

753   The things of this earth are continually passing away: hardly has pleasure begun when it is already ended.

THE WILL OF GOD

754 This is the key to open the door and enter the kingdom of heaven: *"qui facit voluntatem Patris mei qui in coelis est, ipse intrabit in regnum coelorum"*— "he who does the will of my Father, he shall enter!"

755 Many great things depend— don't forget it—on whether you and I live our lives as God wants.

756 We are stones—blocks of stone—that can move, can feel, that have completely free wills.

God himself is the stonecutter who chips off the edges, shaping and modifying us as he desires, with blows of the hammer and chisel.

Let us not try to draw aside, let us not try to evade his will, for in any case we won't be able to avoid the blows. We will suffer all the more, and uselessly. Instead of polished stone suitable for building, we will be a shapeless heap of gravel that people will trample on contemptuously.

757 Resignation?...Conformity? *Love* the will of God!

758 The wholehearted acceptance of the will of God is the sure way of finding joy and peace: happiness in the cross. It's then we realize that Christ's yoke is sweet and that his burden is not heavy.

759 Peace, peace, you tell me. Peace is...for men of *good* will.

760   Here is a thought that brings peace and that the Holy Spirit provides ready-made for those who seek the will of God: *"Dominus regit me, et nihil mihi deerit"*—"The Lord rules me, and I shall want nothing."

What can upset a soul who sincerely repeats these words?

761   Free man, subject yourself to a voluntary servitude, so that Jesus won't have to say of you what we are told he said to St Teresa of others: "Teresa, I was willing. But men were not."

762   An act of complete correspondence to the will of God: Is that what you want, Lord?...Then it's what I want also!

763   Don't hesitate: let your lips pronounce a heartfelt *"Fiat"*—"be it done!" That will be the crowning of your sacrifice.

764   The closer an apostle is to God, the more universal his desires. His heart expands and takes in everybody and everything in its longing to lay the universe at the feet of Jesus.

765   So much do I love your will, my God, that I wouldn't accept heaven itself against your will—if such an absurdity could be.

766   Abandonment to the will of God is the secret of happiness on earth. Say, then: *"meus cibus est, ut faciam voluntatem eius"*—"my food is to do his will."

767   This abandonment is exactly what you need so as never to lose your peace again.

768   *"Gaudium cum pace"*—"joy with peace"—the unfailing and savory fruit of abandonment.

769 Holy indifference is not coldness of heart, as the heart of Jesus was not cold.

770 You're not less happy with too little than with too much.

771 God exalts those who carry out his will in the very same things in which he humbled them.

772 Ask yourself many times during the day: Am I doing at this moment what I ought to be doing?

773 Jesus, whatever you *want*, I love!

774 Steps: to be resigned to the will of God; to conform to the will of God; to want the will of God; to love the will of God.

775 Lord, if it is your will, turn my poor flesh into a crucifix.

776 Don't fall into a vicious circle. You are thinking: when this is settled one way or another, I'll be very generous with my God.

Can't you see that Jesus is waiting for you to be generous without any reservation, so that he can settle things far better than you imagine?

A firm resolution, as a logical consequence: in each moment of each day I will try generously to carry out the will of God.

777 Your own will, your own judgment: that's what upsets you.

778 It takes only a second. Before starting anything ask yourself: What does God want of me in this?

Then, with divine grace, do it!

THE GLORY OF GOD

779   It's good to give glory to God, without seeking a foretaste (wife, children, honors...) of that glory which we will enjoy fully with him in the eternal life...

Besides, he is generous. He returns a hundredfold; and this is true even of children. Many deprive themselves of children for the sake of his glory, and they have thousands of children of their spirit—children, as we are children of our Father in heaven.

780   *"Deo omnis gloria"*—"All glory to God." It is an emphatic confession of our nothingness. He, Jesus, is everything. We, without him, are worth nothing: Nothing.

Our vainglory would be just that: vain glory; it would be sacrilegious theft; the "I" should not appear anywhere.

781 Without me you can do nothing, our Lord has told us. And he has said it so that you and I won't credit ourselves with successes that are his. "*Sine me, nihil!*"—"Without me, nothing!"

782 How can you dare use that spark of the divine intelligence—your mind—in any way other than in giving glory to your Lord?

783 If life didn't have as its aim to give glory to God, it would be detestable—even more, loathsome.

784 Give "all" the glory to God. With your will aided by grace, "squeeze" out each one of your actions, so that nothing remains in them that smacks of human pride, of self-complacency.

785 *"Deus meus es tu, et confitebor tibi: Deus meus es tu, et exaltabo te."*— "You are my God and I will praise you; you are my God and I will exalt you." A beautiful program for an apostle of your caliber.

786 May no attachment bind you to earth except the most divine desire of giving glory to Christ and, through him and with him and in him, to the Father and to the Holy Spirit.

787 Rectify, purify your intention! What a shame if your victory turns out worthless because you acted from human motives.

788 Purity of intention. The suggestions of pride and the impulses of the flesh are not difficult to recognize...And you fight, and with grace, you conquer.

But the motives that inspire you, even in your holiest actions, don't seem clear. And deep down inside you hear a voice which makes you aware of your human motives...so that your soul is subtly haunted by the disturbing thought that you are not acting as you should—for pure love, solely and exclusively to give God all his glory.

React at once each time and say: "Lord, for myself I want nothing. All for your glory and for Love."

789 There is no doubt that you have purified your intentions well when you have said: from this moment on I renounce all human gratitude and reward.

WINNING NEW APOSTLES

790 Don't you long to shout to those youths who are bustling around you: Fools! Leave those worldly things that shackle the heart and very often degrade it...Leave all that and come with us in search of Love!

791 You lack drive. That's why you sway so few. You don't seem very convinced of what you gain by giving up the things of the earth for Christ.

Remember: "A hundredfold and life everlasting!" Would you call that a poor bargain?

792   *"Duc in altum."*—"Put out into the deep." Cast aside the pessimism that makes a coward of you. *"Et laxate retia vestra in capturam"*—"And lower your nets for a catch."

Don't you see that, as Peter said, *"in nomine tuo, laxabo rete"*—"at your word I will lower the net," you can say, "Jesus, in your name I will seek souls!"

793   Winning new apostles. It's the unmistakable sign of true zeal.

794   To sow. The sower went out... Scatter the seed, apostolic soul. The wind of grace will bear it away if the furrow where it falls is not worthy...Sow, and be certain that the seed will take root and bear fruit.

795   By good example good seed is sown; and charity compels us all to sow.

796   Yours is only a small love if you are not zealous for the salvation of all souls. Yours is only a poor love if you are not eager to inflame other apostles with your madness.

797   You know that your way is not clear, and that by not following Jesus closely you remain with that clouded vision.

Then, what are you waiting for to make up your mind?

798   Reasons? What reasons could the poor Ignatius have given to the wise Xavier?

799   What amazes you seems quite natural to me: God has sought you out right in the midst of your work.

That is how he sought the first, Peter and Andrew, John and James, beside their nets, and Matthew, sitting in the custom-house.

And—wonder of wonders—Paul, in his eagerness to destroy the seeds of christianity!

800 The harvest indeed is great, but the laborers are few. *"Rogate ergo!"*— "Pray therefore the Lord of the harvest to send forth laborers into his vineyard."

Prayer is the most effective means of winning other apostles.

801 Through the world still echoes that divine cry: "I have come to cast fire upon the earth, and what will I but that it be kindled?" And you see: it has nearly all died out...

Don't you want to spread the blaze?

802 There is a brilliant man whom you long to draw to your apostolate; there is another, a man of great influence; and a third, full of prudence and virtue.

Pray, offer sacrifices, and work on them with your word and example. They don't come! Don't lose your peace: it's because they are not needed.

Do you think there were no brilliant and influential and prudent and virtuous contemporaries of Peter outside the apostolate of the first twelve?

803 I've been told that you have the knack of drawing souls to your way.

It's a gift to thank God for: to be an instrument for seeking instruments!

804 Help me to cry: Jesus, souls! Apostolic souls! They are for you, for your glory.

You'll see how in the end he will hear us.

805 Listen, where you are... mightn't there be one...or two, who could understand us well?

806   Tell him—yes, *that one*—that I need fifty men who love Jesus Christ above all things.

807   You tell me of a certain friend of yours that he frequents the sacraments, that he is clean-living and a good student... but that he won't respond. When you speak to him of sacrifice and apostolate, he grows sad and tries to avoid you.

Don't let it worry you. It's not a failure of your zeal. It is, to the letter, the scene related by the evangelist: "If you want to be perfect, go, sell what you have and give to the poor" (sacrifice), "and come, follow me" (apostolate).

The young man also "*abiit tristis*"— "went away sad." He was not willing to correspond to grace.

808   "Some good news: a new 'madman' for the 'asylum'."...And all is excitement in the "fisherman's" letter.

May God make your nets really effective!

809 Winning others. Who does not hunger to perpetuate his apostolate?

810 That burning desire to win fellow-apostles is a sure sign of your dedication.

811 Do you remember? Night was falling as you and I began our prayer. From close by came the murmur of water. And, through the stillness of the Castilian city, we also seemed to hear voices of people from many lands, crying to us in anguish that they do not yet know Christ.

Unashamedly you kissed your crucifix and you asked him to make you an apostle of apostles.

812 I can understand that you love your country and your people so much and that still, in spite of these ties, you long for the moment when you will cross lands and seas—far away—for your heart is consumed by the thought of the harvest.

LITTLE THINGS

813   Do everything for love. In that way there will be no little things: everything will be big. Perseverance in the little things for love is heroism.

814   A little act, done for love, is worth so much!

815   Do you really want to be a saint? Carry out the little duty of each moment: do what you ought and put yourself into what you are doing.

816   You have mistaken the way if you scorn the little things.

817   "Great" holiness consists in carrying out the "little" duties of each moment.

818   Great souls pay much attention to little things.

819   Because you have been "*in pauca fidelis*"—"faithful in the little things"—enter into the joy of your Lord. The words are Christ's. "*In pauca fidelis!...*" Now will you disdain little things, if heaven itself is promised to those who keep them?

820   Don't judge by the smallness of the beginnings. My attention was once drawn to the fact that there is no difference in size between seeds that produce annual plants and those that will grow into ageless trees.

821   Don't forget that on earth every big thing has had a small beginning. What is born big is monstrous and dies.

822   You tell me: when the chance comes to do something great, then...! Then? Are you seriously trying to convince me—and to convince yourself—that you will be able to win in the supernatural olympics without daily preparation, without training?

823   Have you seen how that imposing building was constructed? One brick after another. Thousands. But, one by one. And bags and bags of cement, one by one. And stone upon stone, each of them insignificant compared with the massive whole. And beams of steel, and men working, hour after hour, day after day...

Did you see how that imposing building was constructed?...By dint of little things!

824   Have you noticed how human love consists of little things? Well, divine love also consists of little things.

825   Persevere in the exact fulfillment of the obligations of the moment. That work—humble, monotonous, small—is prayer expressed in action, which prepares you to receive the grace of that other work—great and broad and deep—of which you dream.

826   Everything in which we poor little men take part—even sanctity—is a fabric of small trifles which, depending upon one's intention, can form a splendid tapestry of heroism or of degradation, of virtue or of sin.

The epic legends always related extraordinary adventures, but never fail to mix them with homely details about the hero. May you always attach great importance—faithfully—to the little things.

827   Have you ever stopped to consider the enormous sum that many small amounts can come to?

828   It's been a hard experience, but don't forget the lesson. Your big cowardices of the moment correspond—it's very plain—to your little cowardices of each day.

You "have not been able" to conquer in the big things, because you "did not want" to conquer in the little ones.

829   Didn't you see the light in Jesus' eyes when the poor widow left her alms in the temple?

Give him what you can: the merit is not in whether it is big or small, but in the intention with which you give it.

830   Don't be a fool! It's true that at most you play the part of a small bolt in that great undertaking of Christ's.

But do you know what happens when a bolt is not tight enough or when it works itself out of place? Bigger parts also work loose or gears are damaged or broken.

The whole work is slowed up. Perhaps the whole machine will be rendered useless.

What a big thing it is to be a little bolt!

TACTICS

831   Among those around you, apostolic soul, you are the stone fallen into the lake. With your word and example produce a first ripple...and it will produce another...and then another, and another... each time wider.

Now do you understand the greatness of your mission?

832   How anxious people are to get out of place! Think what would happen if each bone and each muscle of the human body wanted to occupy some position other than its own.

There is no other reason for the world's discontent. Continue where you are, my son; right where you are...how much you'll be able to work for the true kingdom of our Lord!

833   Leaders! Strengthen your will so that God will make a leader of you.

Don't you see how evil secret societies work? They've never won over the masses. In their dens they form a number of demon-men who set to work agitating and stirring up the multitudes, making them go wild, so that they will follow them over the precipice, into every excess...and into hell. They spread an accursed seed.

If you wish, you will spread God's word, which is a thousand times blessed and can never fail. If you're generous, if you correspond, with your personal sanctification you can bring about the sanctification of others, the kingdom of Christ, the *"Omnes cum Petro ad Jesum per Mariam"*—"All with Peter to Jesus through Mary."

834   Is there any greater madness than scattering the golden wheat over the ground to let it rot? But without that generous madness there would be no harvest.

Son, how do you stand in regard to generosity?

835   You long to glitter like a star, to shine like a light from high in the heavens?

Better to burn like a torch, hidden, setting fire to all you touch. That's your apostolate; that's why you are on earth.

836   To serve as a loud-speaker for the enemy is the height of idiocy. And if the enemy is an enemy of God, it's a great sin. That's why, in the professional field, I'll never praise the knowledge of those who use it as a rostrum for attacking the Church.

837   Rush, rush, rush! Hustle and
bustle! Feverish activity! The mad urge to
dash about. Amazing material structures...

On the spiritual level...shams, illusions:
flimsy backdrops, cheesecloth scenery,
painted cardboard...Hustle and bustle!
And a lot of people running hither and
thither.

It is because they work thinking only
of "today"; their vision is limited to "the
present". But you must see things with the
eyes of eternity, "keeping in the present"
what has passed and what has yet to come.

Calmness. Peace. Intense life within
you. Without that wild hurry. Without that
mad urge for change. From your own
place in life, like a powerful generator of
spiritual energy, you will give light and
vigor to ever so many without losing your
own vitality and your own light.

838   Have no enemies. Have only
friends: friends on the right—if they have

done or have wished to do you good; and on the left—if they have harmed or tried to harm you.

839 Never go into details of "your" apostolate unless it be for someone else's benefit.

840 May your special dedication pass unnoticed, as for thirty years did that of Jesus.

841 Joseph of Arimathea and Nicodemus visit Jesus secretly in ordinary times and in the time of triumph.

But they are courageous in the face of authority, declaring their love for Christ *audacter*—"boldly"—in the time of cowardice. Learn.

842 Don't worry if "you are known" by your works. It's the good odor of Christ. Moreover as long as you always work exclusively for him, you can rejoice at the fulfillment of those words of the Scripture: "That they may see your good works and give glory to your Father in heaven."

843   *"Non manifeste, sed quasi in occulto"*—"Not publicly, but as if he would keep himself hidden": thus goes Jesus to the feast of Tabernacles.

Thus will he go on the way to Emmaus with Cleophas and his companion. Thus will he be seen after his resurrection by Mary Magdalene.

And thus will he appear—*"non tamen cognoverunt discipuli quia Iesus est"*— "the disciples did not know it was Jesus"—at the miraculous draught of fishes, as St John tells us.

And more hidden still, through love for men, is he in the host.

844   Raise magnificent buildings? Construct sumptuous palaces? Let others raise them. Let others construct them.

Souls! Let us give life to souls—for those buildings and for those palaces!

What fine dwellings are being prepared for us!

845 How you made me laugh, and how you made me think, with that trite remark of yours: I'm all for first things first.

846 Agreed: you do better work with that friendly chat or that heart-to-heart conversation than with making speeches—spectacle! display!—in public before thousands of people.

Nevertheless, when speeches have to be made, make them.

847 The efforts of each one of you individually have little effect. But if you're united by the charity of Christ you'll be amazed at their effectiveness.

848   You want to be a martyr. I'll place a martyrdom within your reach: to be an apostle and not call yourself an apostle, to be a missionary—with a mission—and not call yourself a missionary, to be a man of God and to seem a man of the world: to pass unnoticed!

849   Come on! Ridicule him! Tell him he's behind the times: it's incredible that there are still people who insist on regarding the stagecoach as a good means of transportation. That's for those who dig up musty, old fashioned "Voltairianisms" or discredited liberal ideas of the nineteenth century.

850   What conversations! What vulgarity and what dirt! And you have to associate with them, in the office, in the university, in the operating room...in the world.

If you ask them kindly to shut up, they laugh at you. If you look annoyed, they persist. If you leave them, they continue.

The solution is this: first, pray for them and offer up some sacrifice; then face them like a man and make use of the "strong-language apostolate". When I see you I'll tell you—privately—some useful expressions.

851   Let's channel the "providential imprudence" of youth.

SPIRITUAL CHILDHOOD

852 Try to know the "way of spiritual childhood" without forcing yourself to follow this path. Let the Holy Spirit work in you.

853 The way of childhood. Abandonment. Spiritual childhood. All this is not utter nonsense, but a sturdy and solid christian life.

854 In the spiritual life of childhood the things which the "children" say or do are never puerile or childish.

855 Spiritual childhood is not spiritual foolishness or softness; it is a sane and forceful way which, due to its difficult easiness, the soul must begin and then continue, led by the hand of God.

856   Spiritual childhood demands submission of the mind, which is harder than submission of the will. In order to subject our mind we need not only God's grace, but a continual exercise of our will as well, denying the intellect over and over again, just as it says "no" to the flesh. And so we have the paradox that whoever wants to follow this "little way" in order to become a child, needs to add strength and manliness to his will.

857   To be little. The great daring is always that of children. Who cries for the moon? Who won't stop at danger to get what he wants?

Put in such a child a great deal of God's grace, the desire to do God's will, a great love for Jesus and all the human knowledge he is capable of acquiring, and you'll have a likeness of the apostles of today just as God undoubtedly wants them.

858 Be a child. Even more than you are. But don't stay in the show-off age: have you ever seen anything sillier than a little lad acting like a "big fellow" or a grown man acting like a baby?

A child, with God: and because of that, very much a man in everything else. Ah! and drop those bad habits of a whimpering lap dog.

859 Sometimes we feel the urge to act as little children. What we do then has a wonderful value in God's eyes and, as long as we don't let routine creep in, our "little" works will indeed be fruitful, just as love is always fruitful.

860 Before God, who is eternal, you are a smaller child than, in your sight, a two-year-old toddler.

And besides being a child, you are a child of God. Don't forget it.

861   Child, set yourself on fire with desires to make up for the excesses of your adult life.

862   Foolish child, the day you hide some part of your soul from your director, you will have ceased to be a child, for you will have lost your simplicity.

863   Child, when you really are one, you will be all-powerful.

864   Being a child, you'll have no cares; children quickly forget what troubles them and return to their usual games. With abandonment, therefore, you won't have to worry, for you will rest in the Father.

865   Child, each day offer him... even your frailties.

866 Good child, offer him the work of those neighbors of yours who don't know him; offer him the natural joy of those poor little ones who are brought up in godless schools.

867 Children have nothing of their own; everything belongs to their parents... And your Father always knows very well how to manage the household.

868 Be little, very little. Don't be more than two years old, three at the most. For older children are little rascals who already want to deceive their parents with unbelievable lies.

This is because they have the *fomes*, the inclination to evil, the prelude to sin, but still lack the real experience of evil which will teach them the "science" of sinning and show them how to cover the falseness of their deceits with an appearance of truth.

They have lost their simplicity, and without simplicity it is impossible to be a child before God.

869   But child, why do you insist on walking on stilts?

870   Don't try to be older. A child, always a child, even when you are dying of old age. When a child stumbles and falls, nobody is surprised, and his father promptly picks him up.

When the person who stumbles and falls is older, the immediate reaction is one of laughter. Sometimes, after this first impulse, the laughter gives way to pity. But older people have to get up by themselves.

Your sad experience is that each day is full of stumbles and falls. What would become of you if you were not continually more of a child?

Don't try to be older. Be a child, and when you stumble, may your Father God pick you up by the hand.

871 Child, abandonment demands docility.

872 Don't forget that our Lord has a predilection for little children and for those who become as little children.

873 Paradoxes of a little soul. When Jesus sends you what the world calls good luck, feel sorrow in your heart at the thought of his goodness and of your wickedness. When Jesus sends you what people consider bad luck, rejoice in your heart, for he always gives you what is best. This is the beautiful moment to love the cross.

874 Daring child, cry out: What love was that of Teresa! What zeal was that of Xavier! What an extraordinary man was St Paul! Ah, Jesus, well I...I love you more than Paul, Xavier and Teresa!

LIFE OF CHILDHOOD

875   Don't forget, silly child, that love has made you almighty.

876   Child, don't lose your loving habit of "storming" tabernacles.

877   When I call you "good child" don't think that I imagine you bashful or timid. If you are not manly and normal, instead of being an apostle you will be a caricature that causes laughter.

878   Good child, say to Jesus many times each day: I love you, I love you, I love you...

879 When you feel oppressed by your weaknesses don't let yourself be sad. Glory in your infirmities, like St Paul, for children can imitate their elders without fear of ridicule.

880 Don't let your defects and imperfections nor even your more serious falls, take you away from God. A weak child, if he is wise, tries to keep near his Father.

881 Don't worry if you become annoyed doing those little things he asks of you. You'll come to smile.

Have you never seen a father testing his simple child? How reluctantly the child gives his father the candy he had in his hand! But he gives it: love has conquered.

882 When you want to do things well, really well, it's then you do them worse. Humble yourself before Jesus, saying to him: Don't you see how I do everything wrong? Well, if you don't help me very much, I'll do it all even worse!

Take pity on your child: You see, I want to write a big page each day in the book of my life. But, I'm so clumsy, that if the Master doesn't guide my hand, instead of graceful strokes my pen leaves behind blots and scratches, that can't be shown to anyone.

From now on, Jesus, the writing will always be done by both of us together.

883   I realize, my love, that my clumsiness is so great..., so great that even when I wish to caress I cause pain. Refine the manners of my soul: within the sturdy manliness of this life of childhood, give me—I want you to give me—the gentleness and affection that children show toward their parents in their intimate outpourings of love.

884　　You are full of weaknesses. Every day you see them more clearly. But don't let them frighten you. He well knows you can't yield more fruit.

Your involuntary falls—those of a child—show your Father God that he must take more care, and your Mother Mary that she must never let you go from her loving hand. Each day, as our Lord picks you up from the ground, take advantage of it, embrace him with all your strength and lay your wearied head on his open breast so that you'll be carried away by the beating of his most loving heart.

885　　One pinprick. And another. And another. Suffer them, man! Don't you see you are so little that in your life—in your way—you can offer him only those little crosses?

Besides, look: one cross upon another—one pinprick after another—what a huge pile!

Finally, child, you will have learned to do one really big thing: to love.

886 When a child-like soul tells our Lord of his desires to be forgiven, he can be sure that he will soon see those desires fulfilled. Jesus will tear away from that soul the filthy tail that it drags in punishment for its past offenses. He will remove the dead weight, that residue from all its impurities, which keeps it tied to the ground. He will cast far away all the earthly ballast of that child's heart, so that he may rise up, even to the majesty of God to be dissolved in that living flame of love.

887 That discouragement produced by your repeated lack of generosity, by your relapses, by your falls—perhaps only apparent—often makes you feel as if you had broken something of exceptional value: your sanctification.

Don't be worried: bring to your supernatural life the wise way simple children have of resolving such a conflict.

They have broken—nearly always through frailty—an object that is dear to their father. They're sorry, perhaps they shed tears, but they go to seek consolation from the owner of what has been damaged through their awkwardness; and their father forgets the value—great though it may be—of the broken object and, filled with tenderness, he not only pardons, but consoles and encourages the little one. Learn.

888   Let your prayer be manly. To be a child does not mean to be effeminate.

889   For the person who loves Jesus, prayer—even prayer without consolation—is the sweetness that always puts an end to all sorrow: he goes to pray with the eagerness of a child going to the sugar bowl after taking a bitter dose of medicine.

890   You are distracted in prayer. Try to avoid distractions, but don't worry if in spite of everything you're still distracted.

Don't you see how in ordinary life even the most considerate children play with everything around them, and often pay no attention to what their father says? This does not imply a lack of love, or respect: it's the weakness and littleness proper to a child.

Look then: you are a child before God.

891   When you pray keep the distracting ideas moving, just as if you were a policeman on traffic duty; that's why you have the energetic will-power your life of childhood has given you. But now and then you may retain some such thought for a while to commend to God those who inopportunely have come to your mind.

And then, on your way again, ...and so, until the time is up. When you pray like this, though you may feel you are wasting time, rejoice and believe that you have succeeded in pleasing Jesus.

892   How good it is to be a child! When a man asks a favor, his request must be backed by an account of his achievements.

When it is a child who asks—since children have no achievements—it is enough for him to say: I am a son of such and such a man.

Ah, Lord—tell him with all your soul—I am a child of God!

893   To persevere. A child knocking at a door, knocks once, twice...many times,... and loud and long—shamelessly! And the anger of whoever comes to open is dispelled by the simplicity of the disturbing little creature. So you with God.

894 Have you seen the gratitude of little children? Imitate them, saying to Jesus when things are favorable and when they aren't, "How good you are! How good!"

Those words, said with deep feeling, are part of the way of childhood; and they will lead you to peace, with a measure of tears and laughter, but without any measure of Love.

895 Work tires you physically and leaves you unable to pray. But you're always in the presence of your Father. If you can't speak to him, look at him every now and then like a little child...and he'll smile at you.

896 You think there is something wrong because, in your thanksgiving after communion, the first thing you find yourself doing, without being able to help it, is asking: Jesus, give me this; Jesus, this soul; Jesus, that undertaking?

Don't worry, and don't try to force yourself; when the father is good and the child is simple and fearless, haven't you seen how the little lad puts his hand into his father's pocket, looking for candy, before greeting him with a kiss? Well then...

897 Our will, strengthened by grace, is all-powerful before God. Thus as we travel on a streetcar for instance, if in view of so many offenses against our Lord we say to Jesus with an efficient will: "My God, I would like to make an act of love and of reparation for each turn of the wheels carrying me," then in that very instant in Jesus' eyes, we have really loved him and atoned just as we desired.

Such "nonsense" is not pushing spiritual childhood too far: it's the eternal dialogue between the innocent child and the father doting on his son: "Tell me, how

much do you love me?" and the little lad
pipes out, "A mil-lion mil-lion ti-mes!"

898   If you live the "life of childhood," you should have the sweet-tooth of
a child, a "spiritual sweet-tooth"! Like
those "of your age", think of the good
things your Mother keeps for you.

And do so, many times a day. It's a
matter of a moment: Mary...Jesus...the
tabernacle...communion...love...suffering
...the holy souls in purgatory...those who
are fighting: the pope, the priests...the
faithful...your soul...the souls of your
people...the guardian angels...the sin-
ners...

899   How hard that little mortification is! You struggle. It seems as if
someone were saying to you: Why must
you be so faithful to your plan of life, to
the clock? Look: have you noticed how
easily little children are fooled? They

don't want to take bitter medicine, but "Come on!" they are told, "This little spoonful for Daddy, and this one for Granny." And so on, until they've had the full dose.

Do the same: fifteen minutes more mortification for the souls in purgatory; five minutes more for your parents; another five for your brothers in the apostolate...And so on, until the allotted time is up.

Your mortification done in this way is worth so much!

900 You're not alone. Suffer tribulation cheerfully. It's true, poor child, that you don't feel your Mother's hand in yours. But have you never seen the mothers of this earth, with their arms outstretched, following their little ones when, without anyone's help, they venture to take their first shaky steps? You're not alone: Mary is beside you.

901   Jesus, even if I should die for Love, I could never repay you for the grace you have showered on me in making me little.

CALLING

902 Why don't you give yourself to God once and for all, ...really, ...*now!*

903 If you see your way clearly, follow it. Why don't you shake off the cowardice that holds you back?

904 "Go, preach the gospel...I will be with you." Jesus has said this, and he has said it to you.

905 Patriotic fervor—which is praiseworthy—leads many men to give their lives in service, even in a "crusade". Don't forget that Christ, too, has "crusaders" and people chosen for this service.

906   *"Et regni eius non erit finis"*—
"His kingdom will have no end."

Doesn't it fill you with joy to work for
a kingdom like that?

907   *"Nesciebatis quia in his quae
Patris mei sunt oportet me esse?"*—"Did
you not know that I must be about my
Father's business?"

This reply was made by Jesus the
Youth. And the reply was to a mother like
his Mother, who had been seeking him for
three days, believing him to be lost. It is
a reply that has as a complement those
words of Christ recorded by St Matthew:
"He that loves his father or his mother
more than me is not worthy of me."

908   It is oversimplicity on your part
to judge the value of apostolic undertakings by what you can see of them. With
that standard you would have to prefer a
ton of coal to a handful of diamonds.

909   Now that you have given yourself to him, ask him for a new life—a "seal"—to strengthen the genuiness of your mission as a man of God.

910   Your ideal, your vocation: it's madness. And your friends, your brothers: they're crazy. Haven't you heard that cry deep down within you sometimes? Answer firmly that you are grateful to God for the honor of being one of those "lunatics".

911   You write me: "The great longing we all have to see our work get ahead and spread seems to turn into impatience. When will it get under way? When will it break through? When will we see the world ours?"

And you add: "The longing won't be useless if we use it in pestering and 'coercing' God with prayers. Then we will have made excellent use of our time."

912   I can understand how you are suffering when, in the midst of that forced inactivity, you consider the work still to be done. Your heart would break the bounds of the universe, and yet it has to adapt itself to...an insignificant routine job.

But, for what occasion are we saving the *"Fiat"*—"Your will be done?"

913   Don't doubt it: your vocation is the greatest grace our Lord could have given you. Thank him for it.

914   How pitiful are those crowds— high and low and middle-class—without an ideal! They give the impression that they do not know they have souls: they are a flock, a drove, a herd.

Jesus, only with the help of your merciful love, will we turn the flock into a legion, the drove into an army, and from the herd of swine draw, purified, those who no longer wish to be unclean.

915 The works of God are not a lever, nor a stepping stone.

916 Lord, make us crazy with a contagious craziness that will draw many to your apostolate.

917 *"Nonne cor nostrum ardens erat in nobis, dum loqueretur in via?"*— "Was not our heart burning within us, while he spoke to us on the way?"

If you are an apostle, these words of the disciples of Emmaus should rise spontaneously to the lips of your professional companions when they meet you along the ways of their lives.

918 Go to the apostolate to give everything, and not to seek anything of this world.

919 By calling you to be an apostle, our Lord has reminded you, so that you will never forget it, that you are a child of God.

920   Each one of you must try to be an apostle of apostles.

921   You are salt, apostolic soul. "*Bonum est sal*"—"Salt is good," one reads in the holy Gospel, "*si autem sal evanuerit*"—"but if the salt loses its strength," it is good for nothing, neither for the soil nor for the manure; it is cast out as useless.

You are salt, apostolic soul. But if you lose your strength...

922   My son, if you love your apostolate, be certain that you love God.

923   The day that you really "get the feel" of your apostolate, that apostolate will serve you as a shield to withstand all

the attacks of your enemies on this earth
and in hell.

924 Pray always for perseverance
for yourself and for your companions in
the apostolate. Our adversary, the devil,
knows only too well that you are his great
enemies, ...and when he sees a fall in your
ranks, how pleased he is!

925 Just as observant religious are
eager to know how the first of their order
or congregation lived, so as to have their
model to follow, so you too—christian
layman—should seek to know and imitate
the lives of those disciples of Jesus who
knew Peter and Paul and John, and all but
witnessed the death and resurrection of the
Master.

926 You asked me and so I answer
you: your perfection consists in living
perfectly in the place, occupation and

position in which God, through those in authority, has assigned to you.

927　Pray for one another. One is wavering?...And another?...

Keep on praying, without losing your peace. Some are leaving? Some are being lost?...Our Lord has you all numbered from eternity!

928　You are right. "The peak," you write me, "dominates the country for miles around, and yet there is not a single plain to be seen: just one mountain after another. At times the landscape seems to level out, but then the mist rises and reveals another range that had been hidden."

So it is, so it must be, with the horizon of your apostolate: the world has to be crossed. But there are no roads made for you. You yourselves will make the way through the mountains, beating it out by your own footsteps.

THE APOSTLE

929 The cross on your breast? Good. But the cross on your shoulders, the cross in your flesh, the cross in your mind. Thus will you live for Christ, with Christ and in Christ; only thus will you be an apostle.

930 Apostolic soul, first take care of yourself. Our Lord has said through St Matthew: Many will say to me on the day of judgment: "Lord, Lord, did we not prophesy in your name, and cast out devils in your name, and work many miracles in your name?" Then I will declare to them: "I never knew you. Depart from me, you workers of iniquity."

Let it not be, says St Paul, that I who have preached to others should myself be rejected.

931   St Ignatius, with his military genius, gives us a picture of the devil calling up innumerable demons and scattering them through nations, states, cities and villages after a "sermon" in which he exhorts them to fasten their chains and fetters on the world, leaving no one unbound.

You've told me that you want to be a leader...and what good is a leader in chains?

932   Look: the apostles, for all their evident and undeniable weaknesses, were sincere, simple...transparent.

You, too, have evident and undeniable weaknesses. May you not lack simplicity.

933 There is a story of a soul who, on saying to our Lord in prayer, "Jesus, I love you", heard this reply from heaven: "Deeds are love—not sweet words."

Think if you also could deserve this gentle reproach.

934 Apostolic zeal is a divine madness I want you to have, and it has these symptoms: hunger to know the Master; constant concern for souls; perseverance that nothing can shake.

935 Don't rest on your laurels. If, humanly speaking, that attitude is neither comfortable nor becoming, how will it be when—as now—the laurels are not really yours, but God's?

936 You have come to the apostolate to submit, to annihilate yourself, not to impose your own personal viewpoints.

937   Never be men or women generous in action and sparing in prayer.

938   Try to live in such a way that you can voluntarily deprive yourself of the comfort and ease you wouldn't approve of in the life of another man of God.

Remember, you are the grain of wheat of which the Gospel speaks. If you don't bury yourself and die, there will be no harvest.

939   Be men and women of the world, but don't be worldly men and women.

940   Let us not forget that unity is a symptom of life; disunion is decay, a sure sign of being a corpse.

941   Obedience, the sure way. Blind obedience to your superior, the way of sanctity. Obedience in your apostolate, the only way: for, in a work of God, the spirit must be to obey or to leave.

942 Bear in mind, my son, that you're not just a soul who has joined other souls in order to do a good thing.

That's a lot, but it's still little. You are the apostle, carrying out an imperative command of Christ.

943 Be careful that in dealing with other people you don't make them feel like someone who once exclaimed (and not without reason), "I'm fed up with these righteous characters!"

944 You must inspire others with love of God and zeal for souls, so that they in turn will set on fire many more who are at a third plane, who will in their turn spread the flame to their associates.

What a lot of spiritual calories you need! And what a tremendous responsibil-

ity if you let yourself grow cold! And—
I don't even want to think of it—what a
terrible crime if you were to set a bad
example!

945 You are badly disposed if you
listen to the word of God with a critical
spirit.

946 If you want to give yourselves
to God in the world, more important than
being scholars (women need not be scholars: it's enough for them to be prudent),
you must be spiritual, closely united to our
Lord through prayer. You must wear an
invisible cloak that will cover every single
one of your senses and faculties: praying,
praying, praying; atoning, atoning, atoning.

947 You were amazed that I should
approve of the lack of uniformity in the

apostolate in which you work. And I said to you:

Unity and variety. You have to be different from one another, as the saints in heaven are different, each having his own personal and very special characteristics. But also, you have to be as identical as the saints, who would not be saints if each of them had not identified himself with Christ.

948 Feel and live that fraternal spirit, favored son of God, but without familiarities.

949 To aspire to positions of responsibility in any apostolic undertaking is a useless thing in this life and a danger for the next.

If it's what God wants, you'll be called. And then you ought to accept. But don't forget that wherever you are, you can and

you must sanctify yourself, for that is why
you are there.

950   If you are working for Christ
and imagine that a position of responsibility is anything but a burden, what disillusionment awaits you!

951   To be in charge of an apostolic
undertaking means being ready to suffer
everything, from everybody, with infinite
charity.

952   In apostolic work there can be
no forgiveness for disobedience, nor for
insincerity. Remember, simplicity is not
imprudence, nor indiscretion.

953   You are obliged to pray and
sacrifice yourself for the person and intentions of whoever is in charge of your
apostolic undertaking. If you are remiss in
fulfilling this duty, you make me think
that you lack enthusiasm for your way.

954   Be extremely respectful to your superior, whenever he consults you and you have to oppose his opinions. And never contradict him in the presence of others who are subject to him, even though he may be wrong.

955   In your apostolic undertaking don't fear the enemies "outside", however great their power. This is the enemy most to be feared: your lack of filial spirit and your lack of fraternal spirit.

956   I well understand that you are amused by the slights you receive—even though they may come from influential enemies—as long as you can feel united to your God and your brothers in the apostolate. Slighted? So what!

957   I frequently compare apostolic work with an engine: gears, pistons, valves, bolts.

Well, charity—your charity—is the lubricant.

958   Get rid of that self-satisfied air that keeps the souls around you isolated from your soul. Listen to them and speak with simplicity. Only thus will your work as an apostle expand and be fruitful.

959   Contempt and persecution are blessed signs of divine favor, but there is no proof and sign of favor more beautiful than this: to pass unnoticed.

THE APOSTOLATE

960 Just as the clamor of the ocean is made up of the noise of each of the waves, so the sanctity of your apostolate is made up of the personal virtues of each one of you.

961 It is necessary that you be a "man of God", a man of interior life, a man of prayer and of sacrifice. Your apostolate must be the overflow of your life "within".

962 Unity. Unity and submission. What do I want with the loose parts of a clock—even though they are finely wrought—if they can't tell me the time?

963　　Don't form "cliques" within your work. That would belittle the apostolate: for if, in the end, the "clique" got control of a universal undertaking, how quickly that universal undertaking would be reduced to a clique itself!

964　　"There are so many ways!" you told me dejectedly. There need to be many, so that each soul can find its own in that wonderful variety.

Bewildered? Make your choice once and for all: and the confusion will turn into certainty.

965　　Rejoice when you see others working in a good apostolate. And ask God to grant them abundant grace and correspondence to that grace.

Then, you, on your way. Convince yourself that for you—yours is the only way.

966   You show a bad spirit if it hurts you to see others work for Christ without regard for what you are doing. Remember this passage in St Mark: "Master, we saw a man who was not one of our followers casting out devils in your name, and we forbade him." "Do not forbid him," Jesus replied, "because there is no one who shall work a miracle in my name, and forthwith be able to speak ill of me. For he who is not against you, is for you."

967   It's useless to busy yourself in so many external works if you lack Love. It's like sewing with a needle and no thread.

What a pity if in the end you had carried out *your* apostolate and not *his* apostolate!

968   Joyfully I bless you, my son, for that faith in your mission as an apostle which inspired you to write: "There's no doubt about it; the future is certain, perhaps in spite of us. But it's essential that we should be one with the head—'*ut omnes unum sint!*'—'that all may be one!'—through prayer and through sacrifice."

969 Those who pray and suffer, leaving action for others, will not shine here on earth; but what a radiant crown they will wear in the kingdom of life! Blessed be the "apostolate of suffering"!

970 It is true that I have called your discreet apostolate a "quiet and effective mission". And I have nothing to add.

971 I think so highly of your devotion to the early Christians that I will do all I can to foster it, so that you—like them—will work each day with greater enthusiasm for that effective apostolate of discretion and confidence.

972   When you practise your "apostolate of discretion and confidence," don't tell me that you don't know what to say. For with the psalmist, I will remind you: *"Dominus dabit verbum evangelizantibus virtute multa"*—"the Lord placed on his apostles' lips words filled with efficacy."

973   Those words whispered at the proper time in the ear of your wavering friend; that helpful conversation you manage to start at the right moment; the ready advice that improves his studies; and the discreet indiscretion by which you open for him unsuspected horizons for his zeal—all that is the "apostolate of friendship".

974   "The apostolate of the dinner table!" It is the old hospitality of the patriarchs, together with the fraternal warmth of Bethany. When we practise it, can we not picture Jesus there, presiding as in the house of Lazarus?

975 It is urgent that we strive to rechristianize popular celebrations and customs. It is urgent that public amusements should no longer be left to face the dilemma of being either over-pious or pagan.

Ask God to provide laborers for this much-needed work which could be called the 'entertainment apostolate'.

976 You praised very highly the "letter-writing apostolate". You said: "I don't always find words when it comes to putting down things that might be useful to the friend I am writing. But when I begin, I tell my guardian angel that all I hope from my letter is that it may do some good. And even though I may write only nonsense, no one can take from me—or from my friend—the time I have spent praying for what I know he needs the most."

977   "The letter came on days that were sad—for no reason—and it cheered me up immensely to read and see how the others were working." And another: "Your letters and news of my brothers help me like a happy dream in the midst of the practical realities." And another: "How wonderful it is to receive those letters and know I am a friend of such friends!" And so another, and a thousand more like it: "I received a letter from 'X' and I was ashamed to think of my lack of spirit compared with his."

Now, what do you say of the effectiveness of the "letter writing apostolate"?

978   *"Venite post me, et faciam vos fieri piscatores hominum."*—"Come, follow me, and I will make you fishers of men." Not without reason does our Lord use these words: men—like fish—have to be caught by the head.

What an evangelical depth there is in the intellectual apostolate!

979 It is human nature to have little appreciation for what costs but little. That is why I recommended to you the "apostolate of not giving".

Never fail to claim what is fairly and justly due to you from the practice of your profession, even if your profession is the instrument of your apostolate.

980 Have we not a right to take with us on our journeys some woman, a sister in Jesus Christ, to help us, as do the other apostles, and the brethren of the Lord and Peter himself?

That is what St Paul says in his first epistle to the Corinthians. We cannot disdain the cooperation of women in the apostolate.

981 "And it came to pass afterwards," we read in the eighth chapter of

St Luke, "that he was journeying through towns and villages preaching and proclaiming the good news of the kingdom of God. And with him were the twelve, and certain women who had been cured of evil spirits and infirmities: Mary, who is called Magdalene, from whom seven devils had gone out, and Joanna, the wife of Chuza, Herod's steward, and Susanna, and many others, who used to provide for him out of their means."

I copy these words. And I pray God that if some woman reads me, she may be filled with a holy and fruitful envy.

982   Woman is stronger than man and more faithful in the hour of trial: Mary Magdalene and Mary Cleophas and Salome.

With a group of valiant women like these, closely united to our sorrowful Mother, what work for souls could be done in the world!

PERSEVERANCE

983 To begin is for everyone, to persevere is for saints.

May your perseverance not be a blind consequence of the first impulse, the effect of inertia; may it be a reflective perseverance.

984 Say to him, *"ecce ego quia vocasti me!"*—"Here I am, for you did call me!"

985 You strayed from the way and did not return because you were ashamed. It would be more logical if you were ashamed not to return.

986   "The truth is," you tell me, "that it's not necessary for me to be a hero or to go to ridiculous extremes in order to persevere when I am forced to be isolated."

And you add: "As long as I fulfill the 'norms' you gave me, I won't worry about the snares and pitfalls of my environment; to fear such trifles—that is what I would be afraid of."

Wonderful.

987   Foster and preserve that most noble ideal just born within you. Consider how many flowers blossom in the spring and how few are those that develop fruit.

988   Discouragement is the enemy of your perseverance. If you don't fight against discouragement, you will become pessimistic first and lukewarm afterwards. Be an optimist.

989 Come, now! After saying so often, "The cross, Lord, the cross," it is obvious you wanted a cross to your own taste.

990 Perseverance that nothing can shake. You lack it. Ask it of our Lord and do what you can to obtain it; for perseverance is a great safeguard against your ever turning from the fruitful way you have chosen.

991 You cannot "climb". It's not surprising: that fall!

Persevere and you will "climb". Remember what a spiritual writer has said: your poor soul is like a bird whose wings are caked with mud.

You need suns of heaven and personal efforts—small and constant—to root out those inclinations, those vain fancies, that depression—that mud clinging to your wings.

And you will be free. If you persevere, you will "climb".

992   Give thanks to God who helped you, and rejoice over your victory. What a deep joy you feel in your soul after having corresponded to grace.

993   You reason well...coldly: how many motives for abandoning the task! And some of them are apparently conclusive.

I see without any doubt that you have reasons—but you are not right.

994   "My enthusiasm is gone," you wrote me. Yours has to be a work not of enthusiasm, but of Love, conscious of duty—which means self-denial.

995   Unshakable: that is what you must be. If your perseverance wavers because of other people's weaknesses or because of your own, I cannot but form a poor opinion of your ideal.

Make up your mind once and for all.

996   You have a poor idea of your way, if lack of enthusiasm makes you think you have lost it! It is only the moment of testing: that is why you have been deprived of all sensible consolations.

997   Absence, isolation: trials for your perseverance. Holy Mass, prayer, sacraments, sacrifices, communion of the saints: weapons to conquer in the trial.

998   O blessed perseverance of the donkey that turns the waterwheel! Always the same pace. Always around the same circle. One day after another, every day the same.

Without that, there would be no ripeness in the fruit, nor blossom in the orchard, nor scent of flowers in the garden.

Carry this thought to your interior life.

999   And what is the secret of perseverance? Love. Fall in Love, and you will not leave him.

SUBJECT INDEX

JOSEPH, see St Joseph.

JOY — from 657 to 666; a fruit of faith, 203, 297, 657, 770, 906; of abandonment, 659, 758, 766, 768; and of generosity, 237, 255, 308, 696, 704, 807, 992; its roots in the form of a cross, 217, 626, 658, 660, 671, 672, 692, 758; an always norm, 29, 260, 298, 662-666, 879; sowing joy in the world, 548, 661, 965.

JUDGMENT — 168, 431, 745-748, 930.

JUSTICE — 36, 46, 400, 407, 603, 686, 702; and charity, 449-451, 454, 457.

LAST JUDGMENT, see Judgment.

LAZINESS — 11, 13, 21, 23, 354-358, 935; in the interior life, 325-331; in work, 15, 337, 343, 348; heroic minutes, 17, 78, 191, 206, 253.

LIFE, HUMAN — 135, 224, 297, 306, 420, 692, 703, 752, 753; the meaning of life, 279, 280, 575, 582, 737, 738, 766, 783, 832.

491, 799, 815, 817, 825; presence of God,
277, 302, 359, 545, 772, 778; right intention, 24, 31, 32, 784, 788, 789; practicing
virtues in work, 1, 335, 336, 343, 378, 440,
545, 748; good example, 342, 353, 371.

WORLD, THE — 1, 301, 432, 676, 832, 848;
sanctification of the world, 112, 347, 376,
764, 831, 911, 914, 928, 944.

INDEX OF
SCRIPTURAL QUOTATIONS

*The author quotes the Vulgate version of Holy Scripture. In fidelity to the original text of *The Way*, it has been deemed advisable not to substitute for these quotations of the sacred books the corresponding ones of the recent Neo-Vulgate version.

93	2 Chronicles 7:3; Psalms 117:1
95	Psalms 30:2 and 70:1
96	Luke 11:9
104	Luke 6:12
110	John 3:8
135	1 Corinthians 6:20
138	Romans 7:24
142	Matthew 8:2-3; Mark 1:40-41; cf. Luke 5:12-13
144	cf. John 19:25-27
148	cf. John 4:14
163	Matthew 5:29
183	cf. 2 Kings 11:2-3
199	John 12:24
209	Romans 12:12
213	cf. Luke 22:39-46
216	cf. Psalms 6:7
243	Luke 16:10; John 14:27
244	Psalms 54:13-15
258	Luke 24:36; John 14:27
264	Matthew 9:5
268	cf. Ephesians 5:20; 1 Thessalonians 5:18
291	Matthew 5:48
296	cf. Matthew 27:17-23
300	Matthew 6:24

472	Matthew 6:33
482	Psalms 26:1 and 3
489	cf. Mark 11:33
491	Matthew 13:55; Mark 6:3
502	cf. John 2:1-11
504	cf. Ecclesiasticus 24:24
506	cf. John 19:26-27
507	John 2:1-11 and 19-25; cf. Mark 11:1-10
508	cf. John 19:25
510	Luke 1:38
511	Luke 1:30
512	Luke 1:38; cf. Galatians 4:4-7
520	Galatians 1:18
527	Mark 14:6
536	Matthew 9:12; Mark 2:17; Luke 5:31
538	1 Timothy 6:15; Revelation 19:16
550	2 Timothy 2:10
568	Canticle of Canticles 5:8
570	Acts of the Apostles 12:15
578	Romans 1:17
580	cf. Luke 17:5
584	Hebrews 13:8
585	Matthew 17:19

748	1 Corinthians 3:8; cf. Romans 2:6
750	cf. Ephesians 6:11-12
751	1 Corinthians 2:9
754	Matthew 7:21
758	cf. Matthew 11:30
759	cf. Luke 2:14
760	Psalms 22:1
763	Luke 1:38
766	John 4:34
779	cf. Mark 10:29-30
781	John 15:5
785	Psalms 117:28
791	cf. Matthew 19:29
792	Luke 5:4-5
794	cf. Luke 8:5
799	cf. Matthew 4:18-22 and 9:9; Mark 1:16-20 and 2:13-14; Luke 5:9-11 and 27-28; Acts of the Apostles 9:1-30
800	Matthew 9:37-38; Luke 10:2
801	Luke 12:49
807	Matthew 19:21-22
819	Matthew 25:21
829	cf. Mark 12:41-44
841	Mark 15:43; cf. John 3:1-15; 19:38-42
842	Matthew 5:16

THE NEW TESTAMENT